CHAMPIONS OF WOMEN'S SOCCER

CHAM

Also by Ann Killion

CHAMPIONS OF MEN'S SOCCER

PIONS

OF
WOMEN'S
SOCCER

ANN KILLION

PHILOMEL BOOKS

PHILOMEL BOOKS
an imprint of Penguin Random House LLC
375 Hudson Street
New York, NY 10014

Philomel Books is a registered trademark of Penguin Random House LLC.
Library of Congress Cataloging-in-Publication Data
Names: Killion, Ann, author.
Title: Champions of women's soccer / Ann Killion.
Description: New York, NY : Philomel Books, [2018] | Includes index.
| Audience: Age 8–12. | Audience: Grade 4 to 6.
Identifiers: LCCN 2017037906 | ISBN 9780399549014 (hardback) | ISBN
9780399549021 (ebook)
Subjects: LCSH: Women soccer players—Biography—Juvenile literature.
| BISAC: JUVENILE NONFICTION / Sports & Recreation / Soccer.
| JUVENILE NONFICTION / Biography & Autobiography / Sports &
Recreation. | JUVENILE NONFICTION / Biography & Autobiography
/ Women.
Classification: LCC GV942.7.A1 .K55 2018 | DDC 796.3340922 [B]—dc23
LC record available at https://lccn.loc.gov/2017037906

Printed in the United States of America.
ISBN 9780399549014
10 9 8 7 6 5 4 3 2 1

Edited by Brian Geffen.
Design by Ellice M. Lee.
Text set in 11.5-pt Book Antiqua.

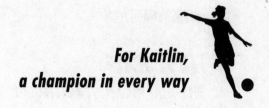

For Kaitlin,
a champion in every way

CONTENTS

▶ ▶ ▶ **PREGAME**

INTRODUCTION

What's the most popular sports team in the United States?

How you answer that question might depend on where you live. Or maybe where your parents grew up. If you were born and bred in Texas, you might love the Dallas Cowboys; if you live in New England, you probably love the Boston Red Sox. Or it could be the San Antonio Spurs or the Chicago Blackhawks or another great franchise. Maybe that's because you live in those cities or because those teams win a lot. It's also possible your parents grew up rooting for them and handed down their allegiance to you like a family heirloom.

Perhaps you like their uniforms. Or your brother hates them and you want to be different.

But those teams aren't America's favorite team. Those aren't teams that get the entire country excited and emotionally invested. They don't make everyone in *all fifty states* pull together and cheer.

But over the past two decades there is one team that has been America's favorite:

The U.S. women's national soccer team!

This team has been astoundingly—historically—popular for many, many years. The team's ability to draw crowds and ratings and become household names has persisted through changes in the lineup and in the coaching staff. Through different World Cup and Olympic cycles. From one century to the next. This team keeps breaking records for attendance and for television viewership—not just for women's sports but for soccer, in general. And it is likely to keep doing so.

During history there have been other very popular American sports teams. For example, the 1980 men's hockey team became legendary for its "Miracle on Ice" gold medal run at the Winter Olympics in Lake Placid, when it beat the powerful Soviet Union.

The 1992 Dream Team—the nickname for the men's Olympic basketball team that played in the Barcelona Olympics—had some of the most famous players to ever play basketball on its roster. Those were teams that all of America cheered for.

But they were mostly popular because of singular

events. They didn't sustain that popularity year after year after year. That's a hard thing to do, because faces change, fans get distracted, national teams play only in certain events and not every week. Interest goes up and down.

The men's basketball players were best known for their NBA affiliations. They were already famous when they put on the USA uniforms. They didn't have to work to make fans.

But the women's soccer team has always known how important it is to connect with their young fans. To bring their sport to different parts of the country. They have always been a team that everyone could cheer for, no matter what part of the country they live in. The U.S. women's soccer team players are best known, first and foremost, for representing the United States.

They are a team that unites America. And can make us proud.

A long time ago, people would have been shocked that a women's sports team could fill the role of America's favorite team. Women's sports weren't considered very interesting or taken very seriously. But the U.S. women's soccer team helped change those ideas forever.

The team first came into existence in 1985, but nobody really paid much attention to it back then despite the fact that soccer is the most popular sport in the world. Soccer was far behind other sports in the United States. And women's team sports were just starting out as something to be taken seriously.

It took several years and a lot of hard work by the players to get noticed and build an impressive women's national soccer tradition in the United States. In 1996, when the women's team won a gold medal at the Atlanta Olympics, it was the first time that women's soccer got any national attention. Onlookers were totally surprised by how many fans packed the stands to watch the team earn the gold medal, with a victory over China.

Not only was the U.S. women's team's rise to the top of the sport amazing, but so was the way fans embraced it. It was an example of "grassroots" popularity, because it started from the bottom and grew upward. Fans found the team and its popularity grew and grew, until finally media outlets and corporate advertisers had to take it seriously. A lot of the sports experts didn't see it coming.

With momentum building, in 1999, the team's

popularity exploded. The U.S. women won a World Cup in the United States by defeating China and captivated the country, selling out giant NFL stadiums and attracting huge TV ratings. It was the biggest women's sporting event in our nation's history. The individual players like Mia Hamm and Brandi Chastain became as famous as many male athletes, which had really never happened for female athletes who play team sports.

Though the players on the roster have changed in the past two decades, the team's popularity hasn't. In fact, it only continues to expand.

In the 2015 Women's World Cup, the final game drew twenty-three million viewers, making it the most watched soccer match—including games played by men—in American history.

Why is the American women's soccer team so popular? It's an especially interesting question because our country doesn't have as long or as rich a soccer history as many other countries.

First, the team has been incredibly successful. Thanks to laws in our country that we will talk more about later, young American women have had many opportunities to play sports. Our soccer team has taken advantage of all of those chances. The players have been very, very talented, winning three World Cup championships, four Olympic gold medals, and one silver medal. The U.S. women's team has been able to sustain success, starting from its early beginnings until today.

In fact, the team is historically so good that everyone was shocked during the 2016 Olympics in Rio de Janeiro when it was knocked out in the quarterfinals against Sweden. It was the first time the American women had failed to advance to at least the semifinals of a major tournament.

Another reason the team is so popular is that it represents something that we all value in America: the fight for equality. The women who play the game have broken down barriers and have fought hard to be treated equally as athletes. They have helped to change ideas about what it means to be a strong, successful woman. They make us feel proud and remind us of what it means to strive for greatness.

Over the years, members of the team have made great efforts to connect with their audience and be accessible, and they continue to work to boost the sport's following by interacting with fans and starting soccer clinics for young, aspiring athletes. They have helped build women's soccer into a national phenomenon, paving the way for future generations of young girls to continue the tradition.

Here's another reason the women's team is so popular: Soccer is a sport that is very similar no matter who is playing it, men or women. In other sports, like basketball, women's teams are often compared to the men's and sometimes that comparison works against them because they're not as tall, they don't dunk as much, and so on. Almost all of the female athletes who play baseball get encouraged to eventually switch to softball, a very different sport. And few women play football at any level. But soccer has the same rules. A match looks the same no matter the gender of the teams playing on the pitch.

This is a book about what makes women's soccer so special. About the most important players—not necessarily the best but the ones with the biggest impact—in the world, both Americans and those from other countries. You might have a different list, but that's one of the fun parts about sports: picking our own favorites and deciding what we value most in an athlete.

In this book, you'll also read about the history of the game and the big events that have shaped it. Included in the stories of the players and important games is also the story of how far women's sports has come over the years. And you'll even learn about the next generation that will carry the sport forward.

These are the champions of women's soccer who have changed the world of sports.

▶ ▶ ▶ **FIRST HALF**

THE AMERICAN STARTING 11

MIA HAMM

Take your victories, whatever they may be,
cherish them, use them, but don't settle for them.

—Mia Hamm

Without Mia Hamm, women's soccer might still have become popular.

But thanks to Mia's presence, the sport exploded.

Mia Hamm is the single most important player in the history of women's soccer. If you were a young girl in the 1990s or early 2000s, you might have had a poster of Mia Hamm on your bedroom wall. Young soccer players coveted the No. 9 jersey, because that was Mia's number.

Mia was the right player at the right moment in time: a dominating athlete, a likable personality, and the best player on the best team exactly when attention was turning toward women's soccer.

She set a standard that continues to be held up today. Whenever a brilliant young talent comes along, she is immediately called "this generation's Mia Hamm." Mia was the top player in the world for a very long time, and she won two World Cups and two gold medals. In her amazing career, she became the most famous player on a team that captured America's attention and respect.

She also represented everything appealing and important about the sport: opportunity for young women, hard work, and a fierce competitive fire. At the height of her career, she was one of the most recognizable athletes in the country. People who knew very little about soccer still knew who Mia Hamm was.

Mia was born in 1972, the same year that Title IX was passed, the federal law that made it illegal to discriminate based on gender. When Mia was born, girls had very little opportunity to play sports. There were few organized youth leagues for girls; high schools and colleges offered limited chances to play sports. What sports were available to girls were often not taken seriously or treated equally. But that started to change thanks to Title IX, the main reason that women's sports were added to athletic programs in high schools and colleges around the country.

Because of Title IX, Mia was raised at a time when she—unlike the women who had been born years before her—almost always had an opportunity to play sports, starting when she was very young.

But even so, early on, it wasn't clear that Mia would ever have a chance to make an impact on the soccer field.

Mia was born with a condition called a clubfoot, which meant that one of her feet was twisted around and was shorter than the other foot. She had to wear special shoes connected by a steel bar at night, and for a time had to wear a cast that helped to correct the physical problem. Eventually, not only did her foot get better, it became one of the most famous feet in all of sports!

When Mia was growing up, her father was in the Air Force, so her family moved around constantly, including to Italy, where she was first exposed to soccer as a very young girl. Because she was always the new girl in town or at school, playing soccer helped her quickly make new friends.

"Sports is how I fit in," Mia once said. "That was my voice. It made me feel good about myself."

Her brother Garrett was also a huge part of the

reason Mia felt like she could fit in. When Mia was five her family adopted her brother Garrett, who was eight. He was a good athlete and when he and Mia played sports with their friends, he always picked his little sister for his teams. Garrett and Mia bonded over their love of sports.

"He never made me feel I couldn't participate because I was a girl," Mia said of her brother.

Mia was devastated when Garrett died from a rare blood disorder at age twenty-eight, never getting to see her play in the 1999 Women's World Cup. Mia created a foundation in his honor to raise money for medical research.

Playing on the field with Garrett and her friends, Mia quickly emerged as an exceptional talent. After her special shoes helped correct the problem she had with her foot, Mia became very fast. She played soccer on boys' teams and also played football in junior high. She was a great scorer in soccer and very competitive. Her family used to tease her because she would get so upset if she lost at anything, including board games.

In 1987, at age fifteen, she became the youngest player ever on the new U.S. women's national team that had been formed just two years earlier. It was coached by Anson Dorrance, the coach of the University of North Carolina soccer team. Mia completed high school in three years, taking night classes to help speed up the process, and then went to play for Dorrance at North Carolina. There she won four collegiate national championships and was teammates with several other members of the national team. She also met her first husband, Christian Corry, on campus.

Mia's work ethic was legendary. One morning, Dorrance saw her running sprints all by herself in North Carolina during the off-season. He sent her a note: "A champion is someone who is bent over, drenched in sweat, at the point of exhaustion when no one else is watching."

It was that kind of dedication and training that would prepare Mia for the big stage.

In 1991, when she was just nineteen, Mia played in the first Women's World Cup, which was held in China. She was supposed to be a reserve, but because of an injury to a teammate, she was moved into the starting lineup. She scored a goal in her first World Cup match, a right-footed blast from the top of the eighteen-yard box, which ended up being the game winner against Sweden. The announcers for the game didn't realize they were witnessing the birth of a superstar. Mia had one more goal in the tournament, against Brazil. In a neck-and-neck finals against Norway, the U.S. team won the World Cup on a timely goal in the 78th minute of the match. Yet despite the thrilling ending, not many people knew anything about it, because the sport was so new for women.

Mia played in the next World Cup in 1995, in Sweden, when she was twenty-three. The Americans finished third in that tournament, losing in the semifinal to Norway, the team they defeated in the 1991 World Cup. During the tournament, Mia contributed a couple of goals and even played goalkeeper for a few minutes in one game when the team's keeper, Briana Scurry, earned a red card for illegally handling a ball, and was sent off.

The next year, Mia helped the United States win gold at the Atlanta Olympics. That was the tournament that convinced the players and the organizers of the 1999 World Cup that the team was popular enough for the event to be held in the biggest stadiums in America. Everywhere the team played, in Orlando and Miami and Georgia, they drew huge crowds full of knowledgeable fans, many waving or wearing No. 9 Hamm jerseys. A then-record crowd of 76,489 filled Sanford Stadium in Athens, Georgia, for the gold-medal match. Mia was hampered by a sprained ankle for much of the tournament but still made an assist on the winning goal to give her team the gold medal over China.

The growing popularity of women's soccer was fueled by Mia. She was the face of the movement. Kids flocked to her, attracted not only by her skill but also by her likable personality. She was the best in the world but didn't act like it and actually tried hard to avoid the spotlight.

Once, when Nike honored her by naming a building at their headquarters in Oregon after her, her teammates teased her by putting signs all over the Nike building: Mia Hamm bathroom, Mia Hamm exit, Mia Hamm drinking fountain. She was embarrassed by all the adulation.

But however hard she tried to avoid the attention, it proved to be an impossible task. At the time of the 1999 World Cup, Mia even made a Gatorade commercial with the most famous athlete in the world, basketball player Michael Jordan. The commercial showed Mia competing against Jordan in all sorts of different sports. A song, "Anything You Can Do, I Can

Do Better," played in the background, as she flipped him over her hip in a judo move. It was a major turning point: for a lot of people, that ad was the first time they even thought about women's soccer.

But in general, Mia preferred to let her teammates, like Brandi Chastain and Julie Foudy, give interviews to the media and star in commercials. As her fame increased in the summer of 1999 during the World Cup, she seemed intent on taking a backseat to her teammates.

Mia was notoriously hard on herself and held herself to extremely high standards. She was full of self-doubt, even though she was widely considered the greatest player in the world. In the scoreless 1999 World Cup final, she asked not to take a penalty kick. Her coach, Tony DiCicco, told her that she was going to have to take one. He wasn't going to leave the world's greatest goal scorer on the sideline while the game was decided.

Mia walked up to the penalty mark, aimed, and fired. GOOD! She made the penalty kick. And after her teammate Brandi made the final kick, the Americans were world champions again.

During her legendary career, Mia became the top

international goal scorer among both men and women. But her record wouldn't last—after all, Mia had opened the floodgates for the next generation of female soccer stars to emerge. After her retirement, Mia's record was eventually broken by her teammate Abby Wambach and by Canadian Christine Sinclair.

Mia was one of the founding members of the Women's United Soccer Association (WUSA), a professional league that was born in 2000 and lasted three years. It folded just days before the 2003 World Cup was about to begin, because of funding problems.

Mia played in that 2003 World Cup and the Athens Olympics the next year. She retired from the national team in 2004, shortly after winning another gold medal in Athens to cap off her incredible career. In 2013, she became the first woman inducted into the World Football Hall of Fame, in Pachuca, Mexico.

She is currently married to former baseball star Nomar Garciaparra. The couple has three children, twin girls and a young son, and they live in Southern California. She continues to be active in soccer ventures, acting as an ambassador for the sport and helping—through her foundation—to bring soccer to underserved communities.

Many people believe Mia was the most important athlete of her era—one of the most important in history—because she changed the country's perceptions of female athletes and what they can accomplish. There's no doubt that Mia Hamm helped usher in a golden age of women's soccer in America. Mia was the face of women's soccer.

STATISTICS:

Position: forward

Two-time World Cup champion (1991, 1999)

Two-time Olympic gold medalist (1996, 2004), silver medalist (2000)

275 appearances for the U.S. national team

158 goals

ABBY WAMBACH

*Every time you fall down, it gives you an
opportunity to question yourself, question your
integrity. It's not about the actual failure . . .
it's about how you respond to it.*

—Abby Wambach

The youngest of seven kids, Abby Wambach was
always looking for extra attention when she was
growing up.

She found it on the soccer field.

Abby became one of the most dangerous scorers
the women's game has ever seen. And, as a result, she
drew everybody's attention: opponents, coaches, fans.
The world!

Abby scored the most goals in the history of
women's international play: 184. Her emergence as the
team's biggest star in the mid-2000s took the women's
game to a new level.

While the dominance of the 1999 team had been

wrapped in a certain grace and finesse, Abby's game represented pure force. Power and muscle. Her trademark move—rising high in the air and hammering the ball into the net with her head—had about as much finesse as a jackhammer.

Raised in upstate New York, Abby discovered soccer as a small child.

"The truth is, I've been on a team my whole life," Abby said. "I'm the youngest of seven."

Abby was toughened up by being used as a target for her older brothers' hockey shots, or as a tackling dummy. She carried that toughness onto the soccer field. She scored so many goals for her five-year-old-girls' team that she was quickly transferred to a boys' team.

In high school, Abby scored 142 goals and led her team to the New York state championship final, which her team lost. She was devastated and blamed herself. But by the time she graduated, the accolades and awards were stacked as high as her overall goal total.

She was a *Parade* High School All-American and voted player of the year by several groups, including an association of soccer coaches. She was a regular in U.S. Soccer's Olympic Development Program, which pulls the top players from each region. And she was one of the country's top ten college recruits.

Abby selected a college that wasn't yet on the soccer radar: University of Florida. The Gators had had a women's soccer team for only three years, yet in Abby's freshman year she led her team to a national championship over mighty University of North Carolina, which was the dominant college program in the sport. Abby also led Florida to soccer's Final Four in her senior year.

Even before Abby graduated from college, she was selected second overall in the 2002 Women's United Soccer Association (WUSA) draft. She played for the Washington Freedom and was teammates with Mia Hamm.

While she was in college Abby began playing for the national team. She played her first game in September 2001 and scored her first goal the next April. She was named to the World Cup roster in 2003, at age twenty-three, despite having played just six international matches. She arrived with a lot of expectations on a team already loaded with stars; Abby's addition marked the most significant difference from the 1999 championship team.

But that 2003 World Cup was a bitter disappointment. The WUSA folded just five days before the opening of the tournament, sending shock waves through the national team, most of whom, like Abby, had been members of the league. The 2003 World Cup was played on U.S. soil after being moved from the original host, China, because of a health scare, but it didn't feel hopeful and exciting like the 1999 World Cup. The players on the national team were crushed by the failure of their league. Eventually, the U.S. team lost to Germany in the semifinals, unable to defend their world championship.

But Abby scored three goals in the tournament, gaining the notice of fans around the globe. The 2003 World Cup marked the beginning of her long career with the national team.

"She's so unique," said her teammate Megan Rapinoe, "in the way that she has dominated. There's never been a player like that."

In 2004, at the Athens Olympics, Abby's true force as a player was unveiled. She scored four goals, including the winner—a 10-yard header off a corner kick—in the 112th minute of the gold medal match. After the game, several of the '99ers retired and, having secured her place as a superstar, Abby became the focal point of the team.

In 2007, the American team went through another heartbreaking World Cup. Under new coach Greg Ryan, the team was a favorite to win. But some of Ryan's coaching decisions hurt the team. In the first game against North Korea, Abby scored a goal to give the Americans a lead. But then she suffered a huge collision with a defender, opening a cut in her head and bleeding profusely. Ryan decided not to replace Abby while she came off the field to get stitches. It was a costly move. Playing a player short for ten minutes, the U.S. team gave up two goals. Abby came back in and the team rallied to tie the game.

The U.S. team lost in the semifinals in that World Cup, to Brazil. Ryan ended up losing his job after the tournament, after a controversial split within the team over his decision to bench starting goalkeeper Hope Solo.

The next major tournament, the 2008 Olympics, was supposed to be a healing time for the team. But it wasn't meant to be for Abby. During a match in San Diego, shortly before the team left for China, Abby broke her leg in a collision. The Olympics were over for her. She stayed home and had surgery to place a titanium rod in her leg. Frustrated by her inability to contribute, she wrote encouraging letters to all her teammates and watched them win gold without her.

It's never easy for an athlete to recover from a serious injury. There's always a question as to whether a player can return and be as good as she was before the injury. Some players simply aren't the same when they step back on the field. Abby was determined to come back better than ever.

After a long healing process, Abby returned to action with the national team and also continued to play professionally in the new women's league: Women's Professional Soccer (WPS). Thankfully, her injury hadn't caused her play to suffer and she was ready to get back to business.

In 2011, the Americans tried once again to win another championship at the World Cup, held in Germany. Abby played a key role in one of the most thrilling games the Americans have ever played, against Brazil in the quarterfinals. Trailing 2–1 in overtime, and playing with just ten players, in the 122nd minute, Megan Rapinoe sent a laser cross downfield, aimed perfectly for Abby's forehead. Abby rose up in the air and banged the tying goal into the back of the net! It was the latest goal ever scored in a FIFA (Fédération Internationale de Football Association) competition and was voted the greatest goal ever scored in a women's world cup.

"That's what the history of this team is about," Abby said. "Never give up."

The U.S. team went on to win that game in penalty kicks and eventually advanced to the final. But the team lost the final to Japan on penalty kicks, and Abby still had never been a world champion.

The 2012 Olympics were eventful for Abby, who was punched in the face by a Colombian player during group play. She ended up with a black eye and swollen face, and the Colombian ended up with a two-game ban. In a rough and physical semifinal game against Canada, Abby used some gamesmanship, counting aloud when the Canadian goalkeeper began stalling for time, trying to get the official to notice, which she did. The Americans were awarded an indirect free kick for the delay-of-game call, and then a handball was called, leading to a penalty kick, which tied the match, and they went on to win. In the championship game, the Americans beat Japan and Abby earned her second career gold medal. Abby was named the FIFA player of the year for 2012.

Abby moved to Portland and married her girlfriend, Sarah Huffman, at a time when same-sex marriage was gaining acceptance. She played for the WPS team in New York. Her career was winding down, but she was still chasing that elusive World Cup.

Abby announced before the 2015 World Cup that the tournament in Canada would be her last. At thirty-five, she felt beaten up and had clearly lost some of her skills. But she wasn't about to go quietly. Prior to the World Cup she spearheaded a lawsuit by a group of women's players against FIFA in an effort to get Canada to put in grass fields for the competition. FIFA requires grass fields for almost all the men's competitions but not for the women. Abby and others argued that it was unfair that they had to play on a surface that contributes to injuries. Despite having tremendous popular support, they ultimately could not effect change fast enough and gave up the lawsuit. But their efforts raised an important issue, which will hopefully lead to greater equality in soccer in the years to come.

Abby, for the first time in twelve years, came off the bench in a couple of games in Canada, including the World Cup final. With the game already almost won for the United States, she came into the game in the 79th minute, taking the captain's armband from Carli Lloyd and receiving a huge ovation.

When the game ended, the Americans victorious, Abby found her wife, Sarah, in the stands and kissed her. That image was beamed around the world, just a few days after same-sex marriage became legal in the United States.

Abby Wambach was finally a World Cup champion.

After the game, during the team's victory tour, Abby announced her official retirement from soccer. She pursued business opportunities and speaking engagements but was struggling with personal problems, including the end of her marriage and a growing dependency on alcohol. In April, a few months after her retirement, Abby was arrested for drunk driving. She wrote an apology to her fans and used the incident as motivation to get sober. She wrote about her battles extensively in her memoir, *Forward*.

Abby's record of 184 goals may never be touched. The most goals scored by a man in international play is 109, by Iran's Ali Daei. Canada's Christine Sinclair is in second place behind Abby with 165 goals. Of Abby's 184 goals, 77 were scored with her head.

And the image of a dominant force, rising up above the goalkeeper to head the ball in, will always be part of Abby's legacy and the lore of the women's national team.

"There's no other player that I can think of, aside from Mia Hamm, that has had such an impact," said Becky Sauerbrunn. "She's just one of those players that demands and commands attention."

Abby got attention. Plenty of it.

STATISTICS:

Position: forward

World Cup champion (2015), runner-up (2011)

Two-time Olympic gold medalist (2004, 2012)

255 appearances for the U.S. national team

184 goals

MICHELLE AKERS

I think the challenge is to take difficult and painful
times and turn them into something beneficial,
something that makes you grow.

—Michelle Akers

Every important movement starts with someone who made the difference.

And the difference-maker in American women's soccer was Michelle Akers.

"She was the best ever," said the late U.S. soccer coach Tony DiCicco. "Because of her strength, athleticism, and skill."

Akers was there at the beginning: the first star of the national team. Though she was ultimately eclipsed by her younger and more famous teammates, particularly Mia Hamm, what the U.S. national team built was constructed on the foundation that Michelle laid down in the early years.

As a little girl, Michelle wanted to play football for the Pittsburgh Steelers. When she was told girls couldn't play American football, first she cried. Then she turned to soccer at age eight. She was very good, very competitive, and very aggressive—so much so that other parents got upset when she was too physical with their daughters.

Michelle was born in 1966, so organized athletics weren't as available to her as they eventually would be to girls who were born later. Society's ideas about girls playing sports were much different when she was growing up. Girls weren't supposed to be tough or aggressive. Back then women were still considered too fragile for the physical demands of sports. Michelle challenged those ideas with her aggressive style of play.

Her introduction to soccer was as a goalkeeper, but Michelle was eager to get involved in the onfield action. She tried to copy men's Brazilian soccer legend Pelé and learned to juggle the ball. She became more and more skilled, and taller and bigger. When Michelle was in high school, she intimidated other kids because of her power and muscles. Her stepmom, Sue, was a coach and a referee and became one of her biggest advocates, instilling in Michelle a belief that she could become a tremendously talented athlete.

Michelle went to college at Central Florida in the early days of organized women's collegiate soccer and earned the first national player of the year award. A year later, in 1985, she joined the first women's national team. She wasn't even sure what a national team was, but if it meant playing soccer, she was interested. Her coach had the players sing "The Star-Spangled Banner" to emphasize what they represented.

With her new teammates she found like-minded athletes who matched her competitiveness and aggressiveness. She scored a goal in her second international match, the second goal ever scored by the United States national team.

Three months before the first Women's World Cup in 1991, during a practice, Michelle slid into a sprinkler head and cut open her knee. She needed thirty-five stitches. But some stitches weren't going to stop her from competing at this history-making event. It was a good thing, too: at the World Cup in China, she scored ten goals in six games.

She scored the winning goal of the first World Cup championship when a Norwegian defender, pressured by Michelle, passed back to her goalkeeper. The pass was soft and Michelle jumped on the ball and knocked it into the wide-open goal.

"It's the goal you think about as a kid," Michelle said. "Last few seconds of the game, open goal, defenders are rushing down, the whole world is watching: Can you score? It was like that. And I did it."

Though much of the American public wasn't paying attention to that first World Cup, the soccer world noticed. Michelle became proof to many that women could play soccer at a high level. Even her childhood hero, Pelé, told the press that he thought she was fantastic.

Mia Hamm, who inherited the title as best player in the game, summed up Michelle in one short sentence:

"She is our everything," Mia said.

Despite her head start as the force behind women's soccer, Michelle had a major setback not long after the first World Cup. She started to feel tired all the time. She was weak and sick, and battling migraine headaches. For three years she struggled with an undiagnosed, strange illness. In 1994 she was diagnosed with chronic fatigue syndrome, a little-understood disease that strikes many people, causing them to be tired often, which makes even day-to-day tasks hard to perform.

Michelle continued to play soccer, but it was difficult playing with less energy than she was used to. She played in the 1995 World Cup, with coaches limiting her minutes. She was named the tournament's MVP. But she was in a constant struggle.

"What you thought you were is stripped away," she said, adding, "You choose how to respond, choose the attitude you will take. You realize you are not a victim. You choose to live."

Around the same time, she also went through a divorce. Michelle turned to her church and her faith to help her cope.

To deal with her physical challenges, she changed her diet and therapy before the 1996 Olympics and was able to play for ninety minutes in four of the team's five matches. Her efforts helped lead the U.S. team to gold.

At the 1999 World Cup, held in her own country and the culmination of all she had fought for and worked for, Michelle was thirty-three years old. Her younger teammates worshipped her. They called her Mufasa—from *The Lion King*—because of her flowing halo of hair.

Throughout the tournament, doctors and trainers managed her health and her schedule, forcing her to take regular naps and monitoring her blood pressure. She was moved back into the midfield from forward, a move designed to preserve her energy.

After every game in the World Cup, Michelle had to get intravenous liquids in the locker room to make sure she was hydrated enough, and thus healthy enough, to play. She continued to insist to her coaches that she could play, constantly telling them, "I'm not coming out." She refused to give up. She knew she could still be a difference-maker.

In the World Cup semifinal at Stanford, Michelle scored a penalty kick in the 80th minute that put her team back in the World Cup final.

In the championship game Michelle was phenomenal, delivering one of the most inspired and—for those who knew what she was dealing with physically—courageous performances in sports. She owned the midfield, controlling the ball and intimidating her opponent on defense, despite her condition and the sweltering heat.

At halftime, the trainers covered her in icy towels. She went back for the second half and continued her dominant play. But she would later say that her mind was becoming fatigued and fuzzy, which was a clear symptom of her illness. The temperatures on the Rose Bowl field soared over 100 degrees. It was an exhausting, stifling atmosphere for even the healthiest players.

"It's the struggle that makes you triumphant," Michelle said.

In extra time, her own goalkeeper, Briana Scurry, accidentally punched Michelle in the head on a China corner kick. She came off the field and put an iced towel on her head as the game continued. Finally, doctors told coach Tony DiCicco that Michelle was done for the day. She couldn't go on.

But could her team succeed without her?

Michelle was led to a medical room in the bowels of the stadium, almost incoherent with fatigue. Doctors cut off her USA jersey and put IV tubes in each arm to hydrate her, and an oxygen mask was placed over her face. She cried, distraught that she couldn't keep playing. Outside that room, on the field, her teammates were trying to win a World Cup without her. Without their foundation.

When Brandi Chastain hit the winning penalty kick, Michelle hugged her doctor. The IV tubes were taken out of her arms and she was helped onto the field to be with her teammates and receive her medal. The crowd of 90,000-plus fans chanted "A-kers, A-kers," and when she got back into the locker room, President Bill Clinton gave her a hug and told her she was his favorite player.

Michelle retired from the national team in 2000, shortly before the Sydney Olympics. She was dealing with a shoulder injury as well as her ongoing chronic fatigue syndrome. When she retired she had 107 goals in 155 appearances.

She didn't leave the team on the best of terms. She had to fight the U.S. Soccer Federation in court over medical bills resulting from the injuries she incurred while playing for the team. Michelle finally prevailed.

After her retirement, she remarried and had a son. She now dedicates herself to the rescue of unwanted horses at her home in Georgia.

On December 11, 2000, a few months after her retirement, Michelle was named the FIFA Women's Player of the Century in the same ceremony in which Pelé and Diego Maradona—the most famous men's players of the twentieth century—were both named players of the century.

If you ask ten people who the best athlete to ever play a certain sport was, you'll likely get ten different answers. But when it comes to U.S. women's soccer, there's no debate as to who was the first. The pioneer. The game-changer.

And to this day, Michelle continues to be an avid follower of the team that she helped start.

STATISTICS:

Position: forward/midfield
Two-time World Cup champion (1991, 1999)
Olympic gold medalist (1996)
155 games played for the U.S. national team
107 goals scored

KRISTINE LILLY

If you care about the people you work with then you work harder.

—Kristine Lilly

Kristine Lilly was a "sneaky" player.

A sneaky player is often overlooked by outsiders, someone who doesn't always show up in the statistics, but one whose teammates consider to be the best player on the team.

The one who is fundamentally excellent.

The person who is always prepared and always takes care of details.

Everyone's favorite player.

For many years on the U.S. women's national team, that player was Kristine.

Shy, quiet, and overshadowed by her more flashy or famous teammates like Julie Foudy, Brandi Chastain, and Mia Hamm, Kristine—"Lil" to her teammates—was the workhorse of the team.

She is the most "capped" player in soccer history, male or female, meaning she made more appearances for her country in international games than anyone else to ever play the game: 354.

Those 354 appearances came during a career that stretched over twenty-three years, starting when she was a teenager and finishing when she was thirty-nine years old.

That's a long career, filled with millions of plays and hundreds of memorable moments. But what Kristine will be most remembered for is one singular second in the biggest game of her life.

In the 1999 World Cup final, the game that cemented the popularity of women's soccer, the United States and China were in a scoreless tie, in overtime. The temperature on the field was soaring. The players were exhausted. The 90,125 people in the sold-out Rose Bowl were on the edge of their seats.

A ball hit an American player and went out of bounds behind the U.S. team's goal, setting up a corner kick for China. Kristine's job was to guard the near post, providing support to goalkeeper Briana Scurry.

The corner kick by Liu Ying arced toward the goal and was headed hard by her teammate Fan Yunjie, powerfully directing the shot toward the goal. Scurry dived to her right but the ball soared past her. For a frozen moment it seemed absolutely certain that China was going to score and win the game. That China would be World Cup champions.

But Kristine—only five-foot-four—jumped high to meet the ball with her forehead and slammed it safely away from the goal. Her teammates corralled the rebound and sent it down the field. Kristine's forehead had saved the game! Her perfect fundamentals helped the Americans win the World Cup.

"She's probably the most underrated player in the world," the late national team coach Tony DiCicco said of No. 13.

Before she became a World Cup champion, Kristine grew up in Connecticut. As a kid, she would often tag along with her brother Scott and their five male cousins who lived nearby, heading to a local field to play sports. They didn't exclude her from football or baseball—she had sure hands and could catch a touchdown or make a play at second base.

When she was six years old she started playing soccer on a boys' team. She didn't have a choice: there were no girls' teams in her hometown. She continued to play with the boys until eighth grade. At one tournament, organizers told her coach that the team couldn't play because it had a girl on its roster. Instead of sitting Kristine, the entire team refused to play. It gave Kristine one of her early glimpses of the power of sportsmanship.

"I was surrounded by guys," Kristine said of her upbringing. "It made me tough. It made me know there was nothing I couldn't do. [My teammates and coach] never said I couldn't play because I was a girl."

When she started playing with girls, she found that she was aggressive, which gave her an advantage.

Those years of training and highly competitive play morphed Kristine into a serious talent. In high school, she helped her team to three Connecticut state championships. When she was just fifteen, she was invited to play on the national under-19 team. Her impressive skills captured the attention of Anson Dorrance, who at the time was the coach of the women's national team and the University of North Carolina (UNC).

She debuted on the national team in 1987, when

she was just sixteen years old, a junior in high school. Can you imagine being sixteen and playing for the national team? While the rest of Kristine's friends were hanging out and going to the movies on weekends, she was preparing to represent her country in the World Cup.

At the time, Kristine also earned a scholarship to UNC, where she played alongside fellow national team member Mia Hamm. Kristine won four national championships in four years and was named the nation's outstanding collegiate player in 1991.

Kristine was proud of these amazing accomplishments, but soccer meant more to her than just winning trophies. When she was a teenager, her parents had gone through a divorce, and Kristine said that she used soccer as an outlet for all her pent-up emotions.

"The only place I expressed my feelings was in a game," she said.

As a member of the U.S. national team, she scored her first goal in August 1987. She scored her last national team goal in May 2010. During her years on the team, she was considered the fittest player and the most fundamentally sound, excelling on both offense and defense with steady, though not showy play.

"[She's] my favorite player," Michelle Akers said of Kristine. "She does the grunt work."

Dorrance, Kristine's college coach, always stressed that excellence meant doing the dull yet important things and making them a habit.

"So many people don't because they don't think it's important," Mia Hamm said. "Kristine does the mundane."

During her long career, Kristine won two World Cups and two gold medals. She played professionally both in Sweden and with the Boston Breakers when there was an opportunity to play professionally in the United States.

During her career, she married Massachusetts firefighter David Heavey. They have two daughters; the oldest, Sidney, was born while her mother was still playing.

After her teammates from the early years on the national team retired, Kristine continued to play for several years, captaining the team into the next era. Some of her younger teammates called her "Grandma." Newer, flashier players—like Abby Wambach—took over the headlines. But Kristine continued to be an indispensable member of the team.

She could do it all. In her long career she scored 130 goals and had 105 assists. She played the most minutes of any player in history.

But her finest moment is one that defined the way Kristine played: it didn't show up in the statistics or the headlines, but that one second in the biggest game of her life made all the difference. Kristine Lilly always showed up when she was needed.

STATISTICS:

Position: forward/midfield

World Cup champion (1991, 1999)

Two-time Olympic gold medalist (1996, 2004), silver medalist (2000)

354 appearances for the U.S. national team

130 goals scored

105 assists

JULIE FOUDY

When people tell you, "No," just smile and
tell them, "Yes, I can."

—Julie Foudy

C an there be anything more important in sports than captaining your team to a World Cup championship?

If you're Julie Foudy, there just might be.

Julie was the captain on the U.S. women's team that changed the world of women's sports forever, the team that won the gold medal in Atlanta and the World Cup championship in 1999.

But throughout her life—her playing career and afterward—she also took a leadership stand on many important issues. She worked hard for women's sport and overall women's rights.

"I was taught early to have confidence," Foudy

said. "That it's OK to disagree and speak your mind in a respectful way. And I learned all those things on the field."

Julie grew up in Mission Viejo, California. She was the Southern California high school player of the year for three straight years. She accepted a scholarship to attend Stanford University, where she helped lead the Cardinal to the postseason in all four years and was named the Soccer America Freshman of the Year in 1989 and Player of the Year in 1991.

Her first appearance with the national team came in 1988, when she was just seventeen. She played in the 1991 World Cup, starting every game in the midfield and playing every minute. She was a hardworking aggressive midfielder who had tremendous vision and poise and the ability to make all the players around her better.

Still, even though there was now an established international women's soccer scene, many people still underestimated talented female athletes like Julie. In 1992, Julie studied in Barcelona. She and a friend found soccer matches that they could play in, but they were treated like freaks. Few people in that soccer-crazed city had seen women play the sport. Clearly the world still hadn't woken up to the fact that women were just as serious about soccer as their male counterparts—if not more so.

After graduating from Stanford, Julie was accepted into medical school but deferred her entry for a year. She finally decided she wasn't fully committed to the idea of a medical career. She was determined to see if she could pursue soccer further.

While she was on the national team, Julie wasn't just the captain and a leader, she was also its social and political conscience. She became concerned when she learned more about American manufacturers of sporting goods using child labor overseas to make equipment. She traveled to tour villages and saw children as young as five years old working in factories. She spoke out and convinced Reebok—her sponsor—to change its policies. She was honored with a FIFA Fair Play Award for her work.

Julie led through humor and chatter—earning the nickname Loudy Foudy.

"I'm a big believer in keeping things light," Julie said of her style. "When we're having fun, and thinking less, and just playing and feeling it—then we're really good."

Julie scored the second goal for the team in its 1999 World Cup opening game against Denmark and immediately struck a pose from an Austin Powers movie that was popular at the time. She helped organize pregame dance parties for her teammates to get the jitters out. On the field, Julie could dictate the rhythm of games. Off the field she helped set the tone and mood for the team.

She was a founding member of WUSA. Her husband, coach Ian Sawyers, whom she met while she was a player at Stanford, coached a team in the league.

In 2000 Julie became the youngest president ever of the Women's Sports Foundation (WSF). Founded by tennis legend Billie Jean King, the organization was dedicated to making sure girls and young women have access to sports and are treated fairly. One of the primary missions of the WSF is protecting Title IX, the federal law that prohibits discrimination on the basis of gender, and advocating for the rights of women.

Julie had always been aware of the opportunities she and her teammates had to play sports, and didn't take them for granted.

"A lot of us called ourselves Title IX babies," she said.

Julie was more than just a figurehead for the WSF. She was fully committed to its cause. In 2002 she was appointed to a commission that was looking into the rules surrounding Title IX and how they might be modified. At the time, the law was under attack from politicians, and schools were trying to find ways not to comply with its rules. Female athletes were still having to battle to be recognized and to be treated equally. There was political pressure to change Title IX, which led to the appointment of the commission.

The commission drafted a report that made suggestions about how to change Title IX, many of which would've hurt sports programs for girls across the country. Julie and fellow panel member Donna de Varona—a former Olympic swimmer—strongly disagreed with the commission's report. They wrote a dissenting report that blistered the perspective that opportunity for women was coming at the expense of prospects for men.

"I just felt that the conversation was always focused on blaming women's sports, instead of finding a solution where we could all play," Foudy said.

In response to the dissenting letter, U.S. secretary of education Rod Paige—who had appointed the commission—said he would only accept unanimous recommendations from the panel. At the end of the process, little changed. Girls' athletic programs in American schools remained intact. Julie and Donna were credited with helping to save the law that had given them and other women so much opportunity.

After winning gold in the 2004 Olympics, Julie retired from the national team, along with other key players.

"I got to play soccer with my best friends for seventeen years," she said.

After her retirement as a player, she still stayed extremely involved in soccer. She embarked on a career as a television analyst, earning strong reviews for her commentary on both men's and women's soccer. She became a journalist for ESPN, covering several sports as a writer and broadcast contributor. She and her husband have two children, Isabel and Declan.

Julie wrote a book, *Choose to Matter: Being Courageously and Fabulously You*. She also founded and runs the Julie Foudy Leadership Academy for girls nine to eighteen years old, which combines leadership skills with soccer.

Patterning on her own life, Julie has found that

leadership skills can grow out of sports. "It's not just sports," she said. "It's teaching young girls the power of sports, helping them become great leaders, needing to unlock that leadership. They're hesitant to raise their hand and use their voice."

Julie made a big difference on the field. She may be making an even bigger difference off the field.

STATISTICS:

Position: midfielder

Two-time World Cup champion (1991, 1999)

Two-time Olympic gold medalist (1996, 2004), silver medalist (2000)

272 appearances for the U.S. national team

45 goals scored

BRANDI CHASTAIN

Never assume greatness is for someone else.
Imagine every day that you too can do great
things. Have the courage to take the challenge,
make the mistakes, and move forward.

—Brandi Chastain

Brandi Chastain wasn't the most talented member of the 1999 U.S. women's soccer team. She didn't play the longest, or have the most goals, or get the most endorsement deals.

But for a time, she was definitely the most famous.

Brandi, who took the winning penalty kick in the championship game of the 1999 World Cup and immediately stripped off her jersey in celebration, became the iconic image for the new power of female athletes.

Biceps bulging as she raised her hands in victory, her ripped torso on display under her black sports bra, ponytail unraveling as she threw back her head in joyful celebration: that image landed on the cover of virtually every newspaper and magazine in the country.

The photo became shorthand for power, for equality, and for a new image of what women could be.

"Everything exploded," Brandi said. "All the emotion, all the work that had gone into that moment . . . it all came together. It was like fireworks."

And they were blinding pyrotechnics. The victory in the World Cup, in front of 90,000-plus people in the stands and a record television audience of almost eighteen million, was the highlight of Brandi's long obsession with soccer.

When she was a little girl, Brandi was a fan of the San Jose Earthquakes, the original team in an old league called the North American Soccer League, a long time before Major League Soccer (MLS) was formed. Her youth soccer team was called the Quakettes. She loved her uniform so much she slept in it.

She went to Earthquakes games and also attended soccer camps where some of the team's players acted as coaches. She learned not only about the game of soccer but also about its rich tradition outside the United States, because so many of the players were from Europe. She became an avid student of the game.

When it came time for college, she accepted a scholarship to the University of California, Berkeley. She was named the Freshman Player of the Year by Soccer America. But a few months later she tore the anterior cruciate ligament (ACL) in her left knee. She lost her motivation and floundered academically. Ultimately, she had to try to find an opportunity to play elsewhere. She tried junior college, and then tore the ACL in her other knee. For two years, her soccer career was in jeopardy.

Eventually, Brandi transferred to the University of Santa Clara in 1989 and, playing on two repaired knees, led the team to the postseason in both of her years there. She played for coach Jerry Smith, who later became her husband, years after she had graduated.

Early on, Smith banished Brandi from the team for having a bad attitude and not training hard enough. After two days in exile she came back, admitted she was "a jerk," and realized that she had to become more of a leader. She used that episode as motivation to improve her character. It turned out to be an invaluable experience. Her senior season, she led Santa Clara to the Final Four and was voted national player of the year.

Brandi was a part of the first national team pool in 1987, but her injuries kept her out of action. Recovered from her knee injuries, Brandi made the 1991 U.S. national team that participated in the very first Women's World Cup. Back then she was a forward and was behind Michelle Akers and April Heinrichs in Anson Dorrance's hierarchy. She played very little in that first World Cup in China, which the American women won.

After that first World Cup, Brandi was dropped from the team by Coach Dorrance's successor, Tony DiCicco. He didn't think she was fit enough, and he didn't feel he had room for her on the team, with the emergence of Mia Hamm. She hadn't been a factor in 1991, so she was expendable. Brandi was devastated. She had played professional soccer briefly in Japan, and in 1995 she sat home and watched her former teammates lose the 1995 World Cup to Norway.

"It was a very hard time for me," she said. "I felt a little lost."

But after the World Cup loss, DiCicco knew he had to make changes to the team's roster. He liked Brandi's soccer savvy and skill, but he told her that if she wanted to make it back on the team she had to switch to defender. That's how she became the starting left back on the team. Brandi approached the switch with intensity, writing down goals, practicing every defensive drill she could find, turning her attention to the great defensive players of the day, like Brazil's Roberto Carlos.

By the 1996 Olympics, she had locked down the spot and helped the Americans win the first gold medal ever awarded in women's soccer. But she was still learning the position. Brandi prided herself on constantly trying to get better.

Going into the 1999 World Cup, Brandi was one of the more visible members of the team. Her teammates had given her the nickname Hollywood, because she liked drama. She liked the spotlight. She gave great interviews. She appeared on the David Letterman show and posed for photos in magazines.

Fitness was no longer an issue; she had worked hard to become one of the fittest players on the team. And she had no apologies about her body.

"It's the picture of a strong confident woman," Brandi said.

But her newfound star status didn't come without some bumps in the road. In the 1999 World Cup,

Brandi had one disastrous moment, scoring an own-goal against Germany in the quarterfinal match in the 5th minute. Yet she recovered to score a tying goal in the 3–2 victory.

In the final against China, after two overtime periods in blistering heat, Brandi lay facedown on the grass, her legs cramping. Her assistant coach Lauren Gregg came over and asked if she wanted to take a penalty kick. And if she did, would she take it with her left foot? The coaches felt she had become predictable and wanted the element of surprise. Brandi, confident with both feet, immediately said okay. She didn't realize she would be the taking the fifth, and potentially final, penalty kick.

With the score tied 4–4, Brandi lined up for the kick. She took a deep breath and pushed her hair behind her ear and swung her left foot, slotting the ball just inside the right post. GOOD! Brandi fell to her knees and ripped off her jersey as her teammates mobbed her.

And Brandi became the symbol of their success.

"Temporary insanity," she said.

Following the win, Brandi became a founding member of the WUSA, the professional league born out of the success of the World Cup. She was a member of the San Jose CyberRays, who played at San Jose State in the same stadium where Brandi had attended Earthquakes games as a girl. With Brandi's help, the CyberRays won the WUSA championship in their founding season, and hopes were high for the success of the league. However, the league folded after three seasons, just before the 2003 World Cup, a stinging blow to all the founders including Brandi.

That was part of a very painful period for Brandi. Her mother, Lark, died of a brain aneurysm in 2002. Seven months later, her father, Roger, died. Brandi was already reeling emotionally when her league folded. Then, in the first game of the 2003 World Cup, Brandi broke her foot against Norway.

"You have a choice in the morning," Brandi said. "What kind of attitude are you going to have? Are you going to be a pessimistic, negative, why-should-I-be-involved type of person? Or 'I can't wait to get out of bed, face the day, what's the next challenge, meet it head on'? That's the only way I was taught."

Motivated to make a comeback, Brandi healed and returned to the starting lineup for the 2004 Athens Olympics. Many of her closest friends—Mia Hamm,

Julie Foudy, and Joy Fawcett—had announced they would retire after Athens. Though Brandi, at thirty-five, was the second-oldest player on the team, she wanted to keep playing. She said her decision was influenced by the personal loss she had suffered and the realization that life is short.

But she never played for the national team after 2004. The new coach, Greg Ryan, flew to San Jose to see Brandi in 2005 to tell her she wasn't going to be included on his team, not even for a tryout. She was disappointed but continued to play in professional leagues for a few more years. She also coached, assisting her husband at Santa Clara and working with a high school boys' team.

In 2006, she and Smith had a son, Jaden. In recent years, she has become involved in various organizations, including one to raise awareness about Crohn's disease, which Jaden was diagnosed with when he was about ten. Brandi has also promised to donate her brain to science, because of her concerns about brain injuries in soccer players, similar to what football players have suffered. She has continued to be involved in soccer and with groups empowering women.

Brandi's epic kick and celebration in 1999 not only

put her on the map, it catapulted the popularity of women's soccer to new heights, especially in America. Every story about her is accompanied by that famous image—the one that changed so much for women, helping to pave the way for the next generation of female soccer stars.

STATISTICS:

Position: forward/defender

Two-time World Cup champion (1991, 1999)

Two-time Olympic gold medalist (1996, 2004), silver medalist (2000)

192 appearances for the U.S. national team

30 goals

CARLI LLOYD

Life is complicated. Life is going to throw all kinds
of obstacles in your way. All I can tell you is what
works for me: be true to yourself, don't do fake,
and above all else, keep on working, because that's
what will take you where you want to go.

—Carli Lloyd

Carli Lloyd has a lesson for you: don't give up.
Many of the most important women to play
for the U.S. women's soccer team were targeted
for stardom early. Mia Hamm was noticed when she
was just fourteen. Abby Wambach was the national
high school player of the year. Kristine Lilly made her
national team debut at sixteen.

But Carli was cut from a South Jersey Select team
at age twelve. She was cut from the regional Olympic
Development Program team. And she was cut from
the U.S. under-21 team, told by the coach that she
wasn't performing to the level of a national team
player.

Someone else might have given up. Not Carli.

And look at her now: she's a two-time FIFA World Player of the Year.

Carli's is a story of hard work, discipline, and persistence. Of working constantly to try to get better. She was born in New Jersey and likes to say that her personality was a product of her state. Like many New Jerseyites, she is not fake. She is honest. And tough. And doesn't give up.

Though she was undersized and—by her own description—an athlete who struggled with fitness, Carli played sports starting at a young age as a way to release her pent-up energy. She played softball and basketball and soccer. Especially soccer.

After getting cut from a select team in middle school, she joined another nearby team and had success, carrying a chip on her shoulder, always reminding herself that the other team didn't think she was good enough. When she was fifteen, she was cut from a regional pool of players in the Olympic Development Program.

But she kept playing. And dreaming. In 1999, she attended one of the World Cup games and brought a poster for her idols to sign. As she watched the

American team emerge victorious, she tried to imagine what it would be like to play at their level.

Determined to see her dreams come true, Carli accepted a scholarship to Rutgers University and, as a freshman, set a school record with fifteen goals and seven assists. That same year, she was invited to join the under-21 team. But the next year the U-21 team changed coaches and the new coach cut Carli.

"I was sure I would never wear a national team jersey again," she said of that devastating day.

But Carli had been in that position before, and she used the setback as fuel to improve her game. Carli changed her commitment to her training. She connected with a trainer named James Galanis, whom she credits for changing her attitude, her stamina, and her overall focus as an athlete.

She was quickly rewarded. She made it back on the U-21 team and then got an invitation to train with the national team. She admitted to being nervous training with legends who had inspired her during the 1999 World Cup. But by 2005, after many of the regulars had retired, Carli was an established part of the national team pool. But she still felt like many of her teammates and her coach, Greg Ryan, doubted her ability.

At the World Cup in 2007 in China, with Carli coming off the bench, the heavily favored U.S. team suffered a huge disappointment, losing in the semifinal to Brazil. After the loss, the team chemistry imploded, with many players turning against goalkeeper Hope Solo, who had expressed anger that she had been benched in favor of veteran Briana Scurry. While the controversy split the team, Carli was one of the few people who stayed friends with Hope. As a result, she became unpopular on the team along with Solo.

"I have never been somebody to go with the crowd," Carli said.

Ryan was fired after the uproar and when new coach Pia Sundhage came in, she changed the team's strategy to one that favored Carli's attacking style. Sundhage also seemed to see the future, becoming the first person to tell Carli, "You have all the tools to become the best player in the world."

As it headed back to China for the 2008 Olympics, the team suffered a setback when star forward Abby Wambach broke her leg in the final game before the team left to travel to the Olympics. Offensive firepower was going to be an issue in Beijing.

But despite an early loss to Norway, the rest of the

team picked up the slack with Wambach absent, cruising to the gold medal game. In that final match against Brazil, Hope Solo kept the Brazilians from scoring and Carli scored the game-winner in extra time. The two outcasts on the team from a year earlier had combined to win the game.

Yet that gold medal didn't mean things suddenly came easily for Carli. Success didn't come without further stumbling blocks. Around that time, she had a heartbreaking split from her family. In her memoir, *When Nobody Was Watching*, Carli said the estrangement came over issues about her parents not trusting her career decisions. It was a difficult time for her.

Carli, as always, kept working. And she kept improving, too. By the 2011 World Cup in Germany, she had cemented her place as a starter at midfield. The U.S. team made it to the final against Japan, and the match came down to penalty kicks. With the pressure on, and the noise of thousands of screaming fans filling her ears, Carli stepped up to take her penalty kick . . . and missed. Her kick was off the mark, sending the ball high over the crossbar. The U.S. team lost the match.

Afterward Carli said, "The emptiness I feel could fill oceans."

Once again, the setback filled her with even more determination. But a year later, Carli started out the Olympics on the bench as Sundhage experimented with different players in midfield. That didn't last for long, though. In the team's first game, one of her teammates was injured and Carli came in, ready to do damage. She delivered quickly, scoring a goal in that match. She started the rest of the games, adding another goal in group play.

In the gold medal game, a huge rematch against Japan, Carli scored both of the team's goals in the 2–1 victory.

"She proved I was wrong," Sundhage said of her earlier decision to bench Carli.

But Carli still found herself occasionally frustrated with her role. Before the 2015 World Cup, new coach Jill Ellis experimented with where to play Carli, putting her outside. Then during the World Cup, Ellis asked her to drop back and play more defensively. Finally, Ellis moved Carli up into her more comfortable attacking position in the quarterfinals, and Carli scored the only goal to beat China. In the semifinals against Germany, she scored on a penalty kick.

That was just the warm-up to one of the most

amazing performances in women's soccer history. On July 5, 2015, in Vancouver, the United States faced Japan in the World Cup final, the third straight major final matchup between the teams.

Fans had barely settled in their seats when, just three minutes in, Carli buried Megan Rapinoe's corner kick with her left foot. Two minutes later she slotted in another goal to give her team a 2–0 lead.

But the most astonishing goal came eleven minutes later. The U.S. was already up 3–0 by that point, when Carli—at midfield—saw that the Japanese goalkeeper was far off her line. She had always had a strong leg, often practiced long-range shots, and thought, why not? From 54 yards out, Carli slammed the ball with her foot at the perfect trajectory, and it looped over Japanese goalkeeper Ayumi Kaihori and into the net.

Three goals—a hat trick—in a World Cup final! The only other person in history to do that was Geoff Hurst for England in the 1966 World Cup against West Germany. Carli's final goal was awarded goal of the tournament and she won the Golden Ball, which is presented to the best individual player of the tournament.

And six months later, Carli was named the FIFA World Player of the Year.

"I love to prove people wrong," Carli said.

At the Rio Olympics in 2016, Carli scored in the team's opening match against New Zealand and later scored the only goal in a 1–0 victory over a talented French team. For a moment in the quarterfinal against Sweden, it looked like Carli had worked her magic again, with what appeared to be a game-winner. But the goal was called offside and the Americans went on to lose to Sweden on penalty kicks. The defending world champions went home unexpectedly early.

Afterward, Carli tweeted: "This one hurts. I am proud to be a part of this team. I am not stopping and will be more motivated in 2019 and 2020. Back to work soon enough."

As always, Carli was determined to move past her latest obstacle.

The result was disappointing but it was just part of an eventful and overall happy time for Carli. Not long after the Olympics, she married her longtime boyfriend Brian Hollins on a beach in Mexico. A few months after that, Carli was named the FIFA Player of the Year for the second year in a row.

And in 2017 she moved to England to play for Manchester City, saying that a year between the

Olympics and the next World Cup was a perfect time to try something new.

"I'm always looking for challenges and ways that I'm going to be able to push my game," Carli said.

After all, she always has.

STATISTICS*:

Position: midfielder

World Cup champion (2015), runner-up (2011)

Two-time Olympic gold medalist (2008, 2012)

237 appearances for the U.S. national team

97 goals

*current player

JOY FAWCETT /
BECKY SAUERBRUNN

*I would write down three goals per game. After
the game, even if we lost, I would look at my goals
and see if I performed as well as I should have.*

—Joy Fawcett

*Some roles hold less glory. They are no less
important.*

—Becky Sauerbrunn

I s it cheating to pick two players for one spot on the
USA's all-time starting eleven?

Maybe. But defenders are used to having to
share the spotlight. If they ever get it at all.

Joy Fawcett was the best defender of her era, that
of the '99ers. Becky Sauerbrunn is the best defender
of her era, the era of the '15ers. It's difficult to pick one
over the other considering the changes in the game, so
both get the nod.

Unless you win a World Cup with a penalty kick

and rip off your jersey, like Brandi Chastain did in 1999, defenders usually don't get much attention. They rarely score goals, they don't make breathtaking saves like goalkeepers, and consequently they get over-looked a lot of the time.

Unless they don't do their job. Then everyone notices.

The United States has a long history of excellent, steady defenders. The team wouldn't have had such extended success without a top-line defense. Joy pro-vided a calming presence on the backline for seventeen years. Her backline partner, Carla Overbeck, was also a defensive standout. Christie Rampone played cen-terback for eighteen years—she was on the 1999 World Cup team that won the title and on the 2015 team that won the title sixteen years later.

And years later, Becky emerged as the best defender in the world at a time when the women's game was becoming so much more diversified and sophisti-cated. As the talent in the women's game has grown increasingly deeper and more skilled, and players are full-time professionals with state-of-the-art train-ing at their disposal, there is more and more pressure on defenders. Many see Becky as the heir apparent to

Joy. Both players were famous for excellent vision, an innate ability to be in the right place when shots were fired, and a calm presence on the field.

Joy was a quiet force on the early national team. Shy and reserved, she was always willing to abdicate the spotlight to her more flamboyant teammates.

"She did things so effortlessly and with such grace," Julie Foudy said of her teammate.

Joy grew up in Orange County, California. After helping Edison High win four league championships, she earned a scholarship to the University of California, Berkeley, where she was a three-time All-American. She joined the national team in 1987, her freshman year at UC Berkeley, and went on to be a staple of the squad over the next two decades.

She was one of the "original five," playing in the 1991 World Cup with Julie Foudy, Mia Hamm, Kristine Lilly, and Brandi Chastain. Though she played midfield early on, Joy became the anchor of the backline and played every minute for the U.S. team in the 1995, 1999, and 2003 World Cups, as well as the 1996 and 2000 Olympics. She remains the highest-scoring defender the team has ever produced.

Even though Joy didn't crave the spotlight, she

received it, not so much for what she did on the field but off. She was the original "soccer mom." In 1999, when the team captured attention, she had two young daughters, which fascinated the media. Her fellow defender Carla Overbeck also had a young son, and U.S. Soccer paid for a nanny who traveled with the team to watch the three children. It was another groundbreaking situation for the women's team, opening eyes to the reality that women could be successful mothers and great, competitive athletes.

During her time with the national team, Joy not only raised three daughters with her husband, Walter, but also coached at UCLA, where she won a conference championship. She later played for the San Diego Spirit in the WUSA.

Joy retired in 2004 after the Athens Olympics. Her daughter Katey, who grew up with the U.S. soccer team, went on to play at the University of Washington, coached by one of Joy's Cal teammates, Lesle Gallimore.

Joy was elected to the Hall of Fame in 2009.

There's plenty of reason to believe Becky Sauerbrunn will join Joy in the Hall of Fame someday.

Like so many players, Becky started out playing

with her two older brothers, while growing up in St. Louis. Naturally, as older brothers often do, the two boys liked to have "fun" with their little sister. She calls herself their "guinea pig." They duct-taped pieces of wood to her arm so she could play goalie, wrapped her in a blanket like a burrito so she couldn't escape, and tortured her stuffed animals.

"They toughened me up mentally," Becky said. "I'm a bit of a scrapper."

Her brothers did something else that helped shape Becky: they helped her learn to read. Becky, who was a literature and composition major at University of Virginia, is the team's most voracious reader, never going anywhere without a book or two in her bag.

"I want to continue learning," Becky said. "Soccer will only last for so long and I'd still like my brain to function, so it's good to keep exercising it."

Becky is also still getting her education by appreciating all the places she travels with the team. She is often one to organize team expeditions.

In fact, given Becky's academic pursuits and the limited opportunities in professional women's soccer at the time, she didn't expect she would have a career in the sport. She was getting a master's in education when the WPS was launched. She left her program to play with the Washington Freedom. During college Becky had played on national youth teams and had a brief call up to the senior team in January 2008, earning her first cap. But then she went back to the U-23 team and seemed to be forgotten. She thought her time on the Freedom might be the pinnacle of her career.

She was out of the loop when the phone rang in 2010. Because of an injury, coach Pia Sundhage needed a replacement player. Becky stayed with the team through World Cup qualifying and, after proving her worth, was named to the roster for the 2011 World Cup. She played in only one match in Germany but was now firmly in the player pool and was included on the 2012 Olympic team.

Becky had waited her turn for a long time, but by the 2015 World Cup, she was the team's starting centerback and considered one of the top defenders in the world. She started every game of the World Cup and logged more minutes than any other member of the team.

"She reads the game so well," coach Jill Ellis said. "On the field she does just the simple things really well."

In 2016 she was a co-captain on the Olympic team in Rio. She was also a leader as one of the players fighting for equal play, saying she wanted U.S. Soccer to recognize her team's "worth and our value." But despite being a leader, she is overshadowed by her teammates.

"I always kind of float under the radar," Becky said. "That's always worked for me."

It worked for Joy, too. The defenders have been the backbones of their teams, calmly backpedaling to kick a ball safely away from harm. You might not find many highlight videos of their play, because it's so steady and unremarkable.

But without their defensive leadership, the U.S. team would not have become the powerhouse it is today.

STATISTICS:

Fawcett:

Position: defender

Two-time World Cup champion (1991, 1999)

Two-time Olympic gold medalist (1996, 2004),
    silver medalist (2000)

239 appearances for the U.S. national team

27 goals scored

STATISTICS:

Sauerbrunn*:

Position: defender

World Cup champion (2015), runner-up (2011)

Olympic gold medalist (2012)

126 appearances for the U.S. national team

0 goals

*current player

BRIANA SCURRY

A champion is someone who does not settle for that day's practice, that day's competition, that day's performance. They are always striving to be better. They don't live in the past.

—Briana Scurry

Back in the 1990s, when the women's national team was gaining prominence, the team was so dominant and the players were so superior to much of their competition that the team's goalkeeper was almost overlooked.

"It's not like I'm back there smoking cigarettes," Briana Scurry once insisted, though at times it seemed like she really didn't have a lot to do.

That changed in the final of the 1999 World Cup, which—for many Americans who were watching soccer for the first time—was their first lesson on how important a goalkeeper could be to her team's success.

▶ ▶ ▶

Scurry grew up outside Minneapolis, Minnesota, and—as a kid—really wanted to play football. American football. In fact, she did, scoring nine touchdowns as a wide receiver one season on a youth team. When she was in middle school, she tried out for soccer and was placed in goal on a boys' team because the coach thought it would be safer for her. In truth, rushing out to smother shots or diving in front of a herd of cleats wasn't very safe, but it did toughen her up.

In high school, Bri was also a track-and-field star and a basketball star, earning all-state recognition in both sports. Her soccer team won the state championship and she was voted the top female athlete in Minnesota. She earned a partial scholarship to the University of Massachusetts Amherst.

Though her parents wanted her to become a doctor or a lawyer, Bri wanted to see how far her soccer skills could take her. She became the top collegiate goalkeeper in the country and when her team faced North Carolina in the National Collegiate Athletic Association (NCAA) Final Four, she received a compliment from Mia Hamm. She told Mia that she hoped Mia's coach Anson Dorrance, who also coached the national team, was also paying attention. It turned out he was—a week later, Bri got an invitation to the national team camp.

She debuted in 1994 and by the time of the 1996 Olympics, she was indispensable, playing every minute of every match. As an African American, she stood out in a sport that was mostly white at the time. She jokingly called herself "the fly in the milk" and said she was comfortable being the only black starter "probably because I've always been the only one." Bri believed that the high fees for playing on club teams were a deterrent keeping more minority players from getting involved.

Bri's most memorable moment came in the World Cup final in 1999. She had already played every minute of every game and had allowed just three goals in the tournament. She called her performance in the semifinals against Brazil on Independence Day the greatest game of her career. She made six saves, including several direct shots by the talented Brazilians.

But the famous moment was to come a week later.

The championship against China was a scoreless tie that went into penalty kicks. On the third penalty kick midfielder Liu Yang went to Bri's left; Bri lunged in that direction and knocked the ball away.

Later, after the game, Bri was accused of improperly leaving the goal line a split second before Liu kicked the ball, which is against the rules. With the new scrutiny of a sport many Americans didn't understand, Bri was accused of cheating. China took up the cry, saying it was against the rules. In reality, it was a foul that was missed by the official. It wasn't cheating but a bit of gamesmanship.

Bri felt something pull in her hip when she lunged for a shot by the captain of the Chinese squad, Sun Wen, that tied the penalty kick score at 4–4. But the injury would never be a factor because on the next kick, Brandi Chastain won the game with her historic penalty kick.

Though Brandi got most of the accolades and the spotlight, Bri's save had opened the door to the victory. Without the save, Brandi's kick wouldn't have made the difference. In the wild aftermath of the game, there were critics who accused the media of prejudicial coverage for not giving Bri the credit she deserved.

Given all the publicity the American team received after the match, some of the players found it hard to continue to focus on training. Suddenly, they were huge celebrities. Bri was one of them, and her lack of fitness led to injuries. By the next year, when it was time for the 2000 Olympics, she was out of shape, had gained fifteen pounds, and lost her position to Siri Mullinix. Though she went to Australia with the team, Scurry didn't play a minute of the Olympics, where the Americans won silver, losing to Norway in the final match.

Disappointed in herself and the outcome, Bri rededicated herself to fitness, losing the extra weight, and worked hard to regain her starting job. During that time, she also was a founding player of the WUSA, the newly formed soccer league. She played for the Atlanta Beat for three seasons, until the league folded. The professional league helped Bri get back in dominant form, an illustration of why the league was so critical for older players who were long past their college days.

Bri was the starting goalkeeper again for the 2003 World Cup and the 2004 Olympics in Greece, where the Americans won gold. She was a crucial part of the team's success. In the next cycle, Scurry—by then in her mid-thirties—lost the starting job to her younger counterpart, Hope Solo, who had been an alternate in Greece.

But Bri's international soccer career wasn't over

quite yet. At the 2007 World Cup, she was inadvertently part of one of the biggest controversies to ever engulf the U.S. team. Though Bri had not started a game in quite a while, coach Greg Ryan benched Hope for a semifinal against Brazil, choosing to start Bri instead. Unfortunately, Bri's lack of recent experience came back to hurt her—it would be her first and last game back as the starter for the team. Bri had a difficult day and the Americans lost 4–0. Afterward Hope expressed her anger over being benched, and the ensuing divide split the team in half and cost Ryan his job.

The next year, under new coach Pia Sundhage, the Americans returned to China for the Olympics and won gold. Hope was the starting goalkeeper and Bri was the backup. Bri's last match for the U.S. team came later that year, in November 2008.

She played briefly for the WPS in 2009 and 2010. She suffered a concussion in April 2010 in a league game, when the knee of an opposing forward slammed into her forehead. Bri suffered from postconcussion syndrome for several years afterward, with symptoms including headaches, depression, loss of memory and focus, and insomnia. Later that year, she retired, ending an impressive career. Years after she hung up her cleats, Bri was awarded the highest honor in American soccer when she was inducted into the National Soccer Hall of Fame in 2017.

In recent years she has become a spokesperson for brain injury awareness. She testified in front of a congressional subcommittee hearing on the dangers of concussions.

"I, too, have been lost in deep, dark places with my face in the dirt," Bri testified, "and have only recently begun to claw my way back to 'my life.'"

Briana Scurry was one of the toughest fighters the women's game has ever known. Even after soccer, she's still continuing her fight.

STATISTICS:

Position: goalkeeper
World Cup Champion (1999)
Two-time Olympic gold medalist (1996, 2004),
    silver medalist (2000)
173 appearances for the U.S. national team
72 shutouts

ALEX MORGAN

Make sure your own worst enemy doesn't
live between your ears.

—Alex Morgan

Maybe it was the pink headband. Or the lightning-quick speed. Or the fact that Alex Morgan didn't seem much older than your own teammates on your club soccer team.

For whatever reason, in 2011, Alex became a new fan favorite, the next generation's successor to Mia Hamm. Everywhere the U.S. team went, from the time Morgan made her World Cup debut in Germany in 2011 through the next several years, the women's national team was greeted by legions of Morgan fans, all donning her trademark pink headband.

Alex Morgan was born in 1989, around the same time the first American women were forming the beginnings of the national team. She was raised in a world where girls not only could play sports, but in many families they were expected to!

Alex played a lot of different sports growing up in Diamond Bar, a Los Angeles suburb. She liked to play the same sports her sisters did, and for a time she was focused on softball. She played volleyball and danced. She played rec league soccer and was coached by her dad, who watched videos to learn the game. Alex didn't join a club team until she was fourteen, old in the opinion of some people. Her success is proof that focusing on just one sport as a young child isn't necessarily the key to success.

"I wasn't ready to commit to one sport," Alex once said. "I was playing with my friends."

But Alex knew that the other girls and coaches were looking at her as though she wasn't good enough to play at their level because she was coming to club soccer so late. And she didn't make the first club she tried out for.

"I knew I was good enough," Alex said. "But I was missing some skills."

She played soccer and volleyball for Diamond Bar High School and was an all-league soccer pick.

Alex's impressive high school career and her production on the club team earned her the chance to play for the University of California, Berkeley. She tore her ACL in high school but worked hard to get back to full strength her freshman year at Cal.

At the time, Berkeley's team wasn't one of the strongest in collegiate soccer, but Alex helped breathe new life into the program, leading the Bears to the NCAA tournament in each of her four years and twice to the second round. She ended her Berkeley career with forty-five goals, was an All-Academic honorable mention three times, and graduated with a degree in political economy. Gone were the days of playing multiple sports—Alex was quickly on her way to becoming a soccer star!

During her college years, she was called in to play on the under-20 national team. At the U-20 World Cup she scored the winning goal against North Korea. Alex spun away from one defender as she trapped a pass, split two defenders, and was being tackled by another as she struck the ball with her left foot from 20 yards out. She buried the ball in the upper corner of the net! The goal was named the Goal of the Tournament and was a hint of the scoring ability that was to come.

In 2010, at age 21, still in her senior year at Berkeley, Alex was called up for World Cup qualifying matches. All of her hard work had paid off—it was time to make her debut for the senior national team. Because of a surprising loss to Mexico, the Americans were struggling to even make the 2011 World Cup, forced to play two games—one at home and one on the road—away against Italy to qualify.

Though Alex already had three international goals to her name, this moment in Padova, Italy, was when she entered the hearts and minds of many American soccer fans: in the 85th minute of a match that was tied 0-0, Alex was subbed in and finally got her shot to make an impact. She wasted no time. In the 4th minute of extra time, she sprinted down the right wing and scored a timely goal to give the Americans a 1-0 win, paving the way for a World Cup berth. Scoring late-game winners was to become Alex's trademark.

In Germany in 2011, she was the youngest member of the national team and a "super sub," coming off the bench to display her lightning-quick speed at forward. She scored two goals in the tournament, including one in the semifinal against France and one in the final (which the Americans lost) against Japan.

By the 2012 Olympics, Morgan was a starter and, as a reliable goal-scorer, had become one of the most important players on the team. She had emerged as an offensive powerhouse. Earlier in the year she scored fourteen goals during a twelve-game stretch. Her speed and finesse combined with fellow forward Abby Wambach's power and force gave the U.S. team a lethal combination at forward.

"Wambach and Morgan are a nightmare," said the coach of New Zealand, whose team had to play the Americans in the London Olympics. "They're both very good technically, and when you nullify one, you find you can't contain the other."

At the Olympics, Morgan scored two goals in the opening match. The brightest moment came in the semifinal against Canada, when late-game Alex emerged again. In the 122nd minute of overtime, she headed the ball in, getting her team into the gold medal match, where the Americans beat Japan. It was a high point in the budding career of a young superstar. That year, only her second full-time on the team, she led the Americans in goals (28), multi-goal games (9), assists (21), and points (77), establishing herself as one of the greatest players in the world.

Alex spent the next couple of years playing but also battling ankle and knee injuries. In 2014, she married her longtime boyfriend Servando Carrasco, a soccer player whom she met while both were playing at Berkeley.

When the Americans made it to the 2015 World Cup in Canada, Alex was rusty, having been sidelined with a knee injury. She came off the bench in the first two games but soon got the rust off and started the third game of group play and all four knockout games. She scored a goal against Colombia and drew fouls that earned penalty kicks in two games, including one against Germany that ended up being the winning goal when converted by Carli Lloyd.

In the run-up to the Rio Olympics, Alex joined a group of national team players in a fight against wage discrimination, charging that they were treated unequally in comparison to the men's national team.

"To force a change, sometimes you need to stand up," Alex told a reporter. "We're not scared."

The dispute was finally settled in April 2017, when the team reached a new contract agreement with U.S. Soccer. Alex said she was pleased with the outcome and described it as "empowering."

In Brazil in the summer of 2015, Alex scored a goal in the U.S. team's first game against New Zealand. And in the quarterfinals against Sweden she scored the game-tying goal in the 77th minute. But the team lost on penalty kicks, a shocking result that marked the first time the Americans had ever been ousted from the Olympics before reaching the gold medal game.

Professionally, Alex experienced the ups and downs that women's soccer leagues in America were going through. Trying to establish a new professional league is always difficult—most struggle to gain popularity within their first few years and ultimately fail. Alex was the No. 1 overall pick in the two-year-old WPS in 2011—selected by the Western New York Flash—and her team won the title that year. But the league folded in early 2012 and Morgan had to find a new team. She went to play with some of her national teammates on a women's team run by the Seattle Sounders of MLS. When the next version of a women's professional league started, the National Women's Soccer League (NWSL), Alex was selected by the Portland Thorns as part of the national team player allocation. In 2015 she was traded to Orlando, the same year her husband was traded from Kansas City to Orlando to play for the local MLS team.

Though her personal life was more settled with her and her husband playing in the same city, Alex decided at the end of 2016 to go to France to play for Lyon, on a six-month loan from Orlando. The president of Olympique Lyonnais contacted her on Twitter and she ultimately agreed to a contract.

It wasn't an easy choice to make, moving halfway across the world to play in a new league. She wrote an open letter to her fans on The Players' Tribune, explaining her decision. Alex said she was excited about Lyon's commitment to women's soccer. Many European soccer clubs have started women's teams in the past decade and given them access to the state-of-the-art facilities. Lyon was one of the first to make a serious commitment, and the results could be seen in the rise of France as a world power in women's soccer. In the spring of 2017, with Alex on the team, Lyon won the women's Champions League title.

"You have to bring your best every day if you want to earn a starting spot," Alex wrote. "My motivation is pretty simple. I hope that this change will help push my game to another level."

"I have big goals," she wrote. "I want to be the best player in the United States . . . the best player in the world."

STATISTICS*:

Position: forward

World Cup Champion (2015), runner-up (2011)

Olympic gold medalist (2012)

125 appearances for the U.S. national team

73 goals

*current player

HOPE SOLO

I think it's my personality to overcome things,
learn from them and become stronger, both
personally and professionally.

—Hope Solo

No one in the history of women's soccer was more skilled at keeping balls out of the net than goalkeeper Hope Solo.

Yet no one was better at letting controversy into her life.

"I don't believe in happy endings," Solo wrote in her memoir, which was published in 2012. That was a foreshadowing of how her international career would end.

Hope was the dominant goalkeeper in the world for almost a decade. She holds the U.S. record for wins, shutouts, appearances, and starts and a record undefeated streak of fifty-five games.

But almost from the start, Hope's life was shaped by turmoil.

She was born in Richland, Washington. Her father, Jeffrey, was in and out of her life as a child. Her childhood was marked by tumultuous incidents, such as the time her father took Hope and her brother to Seattle, without their mother's permission, and was arrested for kidnapping.

In high school, Hope was an outstanding forward, scoring 109 goals. She led her soccer team, and also her basketball team, to state championships.

Her path to goalkeeping came through the Olympic Development Program team. Though she loved playing in the field, her size and athleticism made the coaches view her as a natural goalkeeper.

She received a scholarship to the University of Washington to play goalkeeper. Hope credits head coach Lesle Gallimore and goalkeeping coach Amy Griffin for her progress in learning the position.

"I had been the forward who won games," she said. "It was a huge mental adjustment to learn that my job was to save games. But the intellectual side also made goalkeeping so much more interesting."

While she was in college, Hope reconnected with

her father, who was homeless and living on the streets of Seattle. They established a bond that would last until his death from a heart attack in June 2007. Hope was crushed by the loss; her father had just seemed to stabilize his life.

Hope first played with the national team in 2000. She was an alternate goalkeeper on the Athens Olympic team, which was the finale for many of the veteran players from the 1999 World Cup. A page was turned after that tournament and the next generation started to take over. Hope became the primary goal-keeper in 2005.

She first gained notoriety in the 2007 World Cup in China. In the team's first four games, Hope had two shutouts and had allowed just two goals. The team was riding a fifty-one-game unbeaten streak, and Solo had been in goal for almost all of it.

But heading into the semifinal match against Brazil, coach Greg Ryan announced a change at goal-keeper, putting in veteran Briana Scurry. Though Bri had been one of the stars of the 1999 World Cup, and the starter at the Athens Olympics, winning gold against Brazil, she was now a backup and hadn't started in three months. But Ryan felt she would play well against Brazil, and some of the veterans on the team encouraged him to give Scurry a shot.

The U.S. lost the game badly, 4–0, a shocking result. After the game, in the interview area, Hope criticized the coach's decision.

"It was the wrong decision," she said, "and I think anybody that knows anything about the game knows that. There's no doubt in my mind I would have made those saves. And the fact of the matter is it's not 2004 anymore. It's 2007 and I think you have to live in the present. You can't live by big names. You can't live in the past. It doesn't matter what somebody did in an Olympic gold medal game three years ago. Now is what matters and that's what I think."

Her comments caused an uproar. Some were shocked that a young player would openly criticize her coach. Most had never heard a female athlete be so direct in her displeasure. Others—including many of her teammates—took her words as a direct shot at Bri.

Hope apologized the next day, both publicly and directly to Bri. But Coach Ryan and her team-mates banned her from playing in the third-place game, eating with the team, or flying home with the team. Hope later said that some of the players most instrumental in icing her out were the core veterans of the team, like captain Kristine Lilly. She was kept on the bench throughout the post–World Cup tour. A month later Ryan was fired.

His replacement, Pia Sundhage, sang the song "The Times They Are A-Changin'" at her first meeting with the players and made it clear that the past was over and the rift needed to heal. Hope became the starting goalkeeper again. At the Beijing Olympics in China, one year after her controversy, she made several spectacular saves, diving to smother shots, colliding with players.

In the gold medal match against Brazil, the team she hadn't had a chance to face a year earlier in China, Hope was the star. In the 72nd minute, Marta—the best player in the world at the time—got past two defenders and shot at the goal from point-blank range. In a rush like a tornado, Hope thrust her forearm into the air to block the shot, sending it safely away. Marta threw up her arms in frustration. The save proved to be instrumental. The U.S. team won the game in overtime for the gold medal.

"It's like a storybook ending," Hope said afterward. "My life doesn't play out like that all the time."

For the next eight years, Hope went unchallenged in goal. She led the United States in the 2011 Women's World Cup, saving a penalty kick in a shoot-out against Brazil, which put her team in the semifinals. The Americans lost in the final on penalty kicks to Japan. Hope helped the United States win gold at the London Olympics in 2012. And she finally won a World Cup in 2015 in Canada.

During those years, she had both shoulder and wrist surgery. Along the way she played professionally in Europe—in Sweden and France—for the WPS and the NWSL. She was named the U.S. Soccer Athlete of the Year in 2009 and twice won the FIFA Golden Glove, awarded to the most outstanding goalkeeper in the World Cup. She also published a memoir, *Solo: A Memoir of Hope*, which became a *New York Times* best seller, and appeared on *Dancing with the Stars*.

But despite all her success, controversy still followed Solo. She was arrested on a domestic violence charge for an altercation that involved her stepsister and nephew. Though charges were initially dismissed, prosecutors filed an appeal with the Superior Court of Washington and the charges were reinstated and, as of 2017, the case remains unresolved.

Five months before the 2015 World Cup, she was suspended by U.S. Soccer for a month for what the organization termed "a poor decision." She was a passenger in a team van her husband, Jerramy Stevens, was driving when he was arrested for driving under the influence.

Though the controversies damaged her reputation in public, and with media critics, they didn't seem to affect Hope's ability to play on the field. In Canada, she was the anchor of a strong defense and the Americans won their first World Cup since 1999.

During the 2016 Rio Olympics, Hope had two shutouts in the first two games, including a spectacular performance against France. However, in the team's third game against Colombia, Hope made two rare errors and was self-critical afterward.

In the first knockout game against Sweden—now coached by former U.S. coach Pia Sundhage—Sweden played an extremely defensive game. The game ended 1–1 and went to penalty kicks, which Sweden won. It was the first time in history that the U.S. team hadn't reached the Olympic final. After the game, in the interview area, Hope criticized Sweden's style of play.

"I think we showed a lot of heart," Hope said. "We

came back from a goal down. I'm very proud of this team . . . I also think we played a bunch of cowards. The best team did not win today. I strongly, firmly believe that.

"But they won. They're moving on and we're going home."

Her comments, once again, caused a huge uproar, overshadowing the team's poor performance. A month later, U.S. Soccer terminated her contract—in other words, they fired Hope. Sunil Gulati, the president of U.S. Soccer, said her comments did not "meet the standard of conduct we require from our players."

While some applauded, U.S. Soccer was also criticized for its action. Some said a male player would not have been fired for the same reason. In fact, superstar Cristiano Ronaldo had said similar things about an opponent just a few months earlier. Others said it was a convenient time for the organization to punish a seventeen-year employee, who had turned thirty-five and might no longer have been the starter by the time the 2019 World Cup came around.

Hope later said she believed she was, in part, being punished for her role in a pay dispute. She was one of five team members who filed a wage discrimination claim against the U.S. Soccer Federation, showing that they were paid substantially less than male players.

"I was a thorn in their side," Hope said.

As Hope herself said, she didn't believe in happy endings. And her finale with the U.S. soccer team brought a controversial end to the career of the one of its greatest players ever.

STATISTICS:

Position: goalkeeper

World Cup champion (2015), runner-up (2011)

Two-time Olympic gold medalist (2008, 2012)

202 appearances for the U.S. national team

152 wins (most by a goalkeeper)

102 shutouts

TOP TEN SAVES
IN WOMEN'S SOCCER HISTORY

10. SANDRA SEPULVEDA, 2015 WOMEN'S WORLD CUP GROUP GAME, COLOMBIA VS. FRANCE

France was a heavy favorite in its group but suffered a stunning setback in group play, thanks in large part to the play of Colombian goalkeeper Sepulveda, who made several big saves. One came against French midfielder Elise Bussaglia, who—aiming to tie the game—hit the ball high. Sepulveda leapt and extended and pushed the ball over the crossbar with her fingertip! Sepulveda continued to keep the French out of the goal and came away with a 2–0 win, considered one of the biggest upsets of the World Cup in Canada.

9. HEDVIG LINDAHL, 2016 OLYMPIC SEMIFINAL, SWEDEN VS. BRAZIL

A wild, partisan crowd packed iconic Maracanã Stadium to support their nation's squad, almost all of them wearing Marta jerseys and urging their team onto success. But Sweden's Lindahl and her teammates thwarted Brazil's firepower and hopes. The game went into penalty kicks, for the second consecutive time for Sweden. The teams were even at 3–3 through the first four rounds of kicks. Lindahl had already saved one kick, which is no easy task. On Brazil's fifth kick, taken by Andressinha, Lindahl laid herself out to her right and batted the ball away. That would be the difference, as Sweden converted its next kick and moved on to the final.

8. TARYN SWIATEK, 2003 WORLD CUP QUARTERFINAL, CANADA VS. CHINA

China was just four years removed from almost winning the 1999 World Cup, and Canada was a team that had accomplished little in its history. But in one of the biggest upsets of the tournament, Canada ousted China, in part thanks to the skills of goal-keeper Swiatek. With dangerous Sun Wen taking a free kick early in the game, Swiatek leapt up and punched the ball over the crossbar, leaving Wen shaking her head in frustration. Canada would go on to win 1–0 and advance to the semifinals for the first time in its history.

7. **HOPE SOLO**, 2011 WORLD CUP QUARTERFINAL, USA VS. BRAZIL

In what is often called the greatest game ever played, the dramatics still weren't over after the U.S. team scored the latest goal ever in World Cup history. That goal, scored in the 122nd minute of the match, tied the game, pushing it into penalty kicks. Solo had not been able to make a save on either of the first two shots taken by the Brazilians. But the third player to take her turn was Daiane dos Santos, who was shaky because she had scored an own-goal earlier in the game. Solo read dos Santos's movements and dived to her right, getting her right hand on the ball and pushing it away. That was the difference that sent the Americans on to the semifinal.

6. SILKE ROTTENBERG, 2003 WORLD CUP SEMIFINAL, GERMANY VS. USA

The defending World Cup champions, the Americans, were favorites, playing at home in 2003. But they ran into a German buzz saw that not only could score but, thanks to the skills of goalkeeper Rottenberg, could also keep the Americans from scoring. In the first half, with Mia Hamm bearing down on her, Rottenberg came out of the goal and got her hands on the ball, getting kicked in the head in the process. But she kept the best player in the world from scoring.

5. BRIANA SCURRY, 1999 WORLD CUP SEMIFINAL, USA VS. BRAZIL

In what Scurry called the best game she had ever played, the Americans won 2–0 to advance to the World Cup final. But it wasn't easy. Brazil was tenacious and Scurry was called on to save her team countless times. In the first half she punched away a point-blank shot, and then she started the second half by pushing a ball over the crossbar. But the save of the game at Stanford Stadium came midway through the second half when Scurry dove flat on the ground to get her fingertips on the ball and knock it away.

4. NADINE ANGERER, 2007 WORLD CUP FINAL, GERMANY VS. BRAZIL

Angerer hadn't given up a goal in the entire World Cup, but it looked like her streak would come to an end in the second half of the final against Brazil. Brazilian Cristiane was tackled inside the box and Brazil was awarded a penalty kick. Marta confidently lined up to take the kick, but Angerer dove to her right and smothered the ball. Her perfect streak continued and Germany went on to win its second consecutive championship.

3. HOPE SOLO, 2008 OLYMPIC GOLD MEDAL GAME, USA VS. BRAZIL

The game was supposed to be an opportunity for retribution for the Americans coming off a loss to Brazil in the World Cup the year before, and for Solo, following her controversial benching in that game. The battle was tense and still scoreless late in the match. Marta came at Solo at full speed, squeezing between two American defenders and getting off a hard shot. A diving Solo raised her arm to block the ball; the impact was so loud the announcers were convinced the ball had hit the post until they watched the replay. The Americans went on to win, 1–0, thanks to a Carli Lloyd goal in extra time.

2. AYUMI KAIHORI, 2011 WORLD CUP FINAL, JAPAN VS. USA

Japan was the heavy underdog in the final matchup that ended in a 2–2 tie after regulation. Goalkeeper Kaihori faced the powerful American shooters in penalty kicks and ended up saving two shots. Of the two stops, the first was the most important, preventing the Americans from gaining any momentum and sowing seeds of doubt. Shannon Boxx went first for the U.S. team. Kaihori guessed correctly, diving to her left, but almost overplayed the ball. From the ground she launched her feet up high and kicked the ball away. The United States was already in a hole and would never recover.

1. **BRIANA SCURRY**, 1999 WORLD CUP FINAL, USA VS. CHINA.

The world of women's soccer over the past two decades could've been very different without Scurry's diving save during the penalty kick shootout at the Rose Bowl in 1999. All either side needed to be crowned champion of the biggest sporting event in women's sports history was one save. Liu Ying was the third Chinese player to take a kick. Scurry lunged forward and dived to her left, pushing the ball away with both hands and hitting the ground with force. She leapt up and pumped both fists as the crowd of more than 90,000 roared. Though there was later controversy because Scurry left her line before Liu kicked the ball, there was no foul called on the field. The controversy faded into obscurity. What was left was that only one penalty kick in that championship wasn't converted: the one saved by Scurry.

▶ ▶ ▶ **HALFTIME**

THE HISTORY OF SOCCER

Women and girls have been playing soccer for a long time. Probably since the early days when people first started kicking around balls on neighborhood fields, on city streets, and in backyards around the world.

But as an organized sport, women's soccer has a relatively short history. That's because, throughout much of the nineteenth century, while men were launching professional sports leagues, women were expected to stay in the home and care for children. When they did attempt to play soccer, or other sports, it was considered too rough, too exhausting, and just too inappropriate for females to play. So even if little girls were kicking a ball around with their brothers, they didn't get a chance to play beyond the street or playground.

Now we've moved on from those old beliefs and realize how silly such restrictions were. But it took a lot of time and progress to get to where we are today.

I. EARLY BEGINNINGS

The first women's official "international" match took place in 1881 between England and Scotland. It was around that time that women's football clubs slowly began to appear around London, a few years after men's teams had been formed.

During World War I, with most men away fighting on the front lines, women went to work in factories, and they began to play on intramural soccer teams that emerged as part of the workplace, just as men had done for years. The sport was popular and the women's game drew big crowds, some reportedly as large as 50,000. After the war ended, some of those factory teams reformed as local soccer clubs.

One, the Dick, Kerr's Ladies (a team that had been started at the Dick, Kerr munitions factory), had a savvy manager who saw a marketing opportunity. The team played eight games against a French team, in contests billed as the first unofficial international matches for women. A reported 25,000 turned out to see England beat France 2–0 in Preston, England, in the first game. Three more games followed in England—played on the grounds of men's clubs—and four in France. All were played before large crowds.

But shortly after those landmark games, in 1921, the English Football Association (FA) banned women's teams, requesting that FA clubs not allow their facilities to be used for women's games. The resolution was passed by members who stated, "Their strong opinion that the game of [soccer] is quite unsuitable for females and ought not to be encouraged." Other national federations passed similar resolutions, all but banning women's soccer as an organized sport around the world.

But as attitudes toward gender and societal norms began to change midway through the twentieth century, more and more women started to play soccer. In Germany, a women's league was formed in the early 1970s, and the women's Bundesliga—a counterpart to Germany's famous men's league—was launched in 1990. In Sweden, the number of women playing soccer boomed in the 1970s and a professional league—the Damallsvenskan—was launched in 1988. In Japan, a women's football association was started in the 1970s and a professional league was officially launched in 1989. All these movements were happening simultaneously around the globe.

While leagues formed in Europe and Asia, the United States fell behind much of the rest of the world in terms of the game of soccer, for both men and women. That was largely because of the rise of American football. And the nation's pastime, baseball, also captured the attention of sports fans across the country. Soccer simply wasn't a part of the American sports identity. But in certain immigrant communities in the United States, soccer thrived and in some of those places, women also played. For example, in St. Louis—where German, Irish, and Italian immigrants all played the sport—a women's league was established in 1951.

It was clear that women wanted to play sports. They wanted to play soccer. And they weren't going to be stopped.

II. TITLE IX

Women's sports got its biggest boost in the United States with the passage of Title IX, a federal law that prohibited discrimination based on gender. President Richard Nixon signed the law in June 1972.

It's a simple statement, just thirty-seven words, but it changed everything for women.

Title IX reads:

"No person in the United States shall, on the basis of sex, be excluded from participation in, be denied the benefits of, or be subjected to discrimination under any education program or activity receiving Federal financial assistance."

One of the main practical applications of the law was to make schools—high schools and colleges—offer sports programs for girls. Boys' and men's athletic programs were a part of the educational experience, and now girls had a tool to ask for the same benefits for themselves.

There were many attempts over the years to change or alter the wording, or to reverse the law. Citizens have had to fight very hard to have the law upheld. But despite the ongoing battles, Title IX, which remains alive and well today, created a major change in opening the doors of sports for girls.

Suddenly the floodgates opened and progress accelerated. Girls could now push for the formation of athletic programs, including soccer. By 1981, there were more than 100 collegiate programs in the United States, and by 1982 the National Collegiate Athletic Association (NCAA) sponsored the first women's tournament. The sport grew quickly around the country and soon surpassed men's soccer in terms of the number of varsity programs. Part of the reason is that Title IX mandates equal opportunity. Because collegiate American football teams field so many players and use up so many scholarships, women's soccer—with more players than most women's athletic teams—was added to help balance the scales.

The University of North Carolina helped put women's soccer on the radar. The university already had a historic sports record, particularly in terms of men's basketball, and it soon became a women's soccer powerhouse as well. Under the guidance of their excellent coach Anson Dorrance, the Tar Heels made waves over the following years, winning twelve of the first thirteen NCAA championships from 1982 to 1994. As of early 2017, they've won twenty-one altogether. Dorrance recruited and coached many of the players who would go on to be the biggest stars of the sport—Kristine Lilly, Mia Hamm, Crystal Dunn, Tobin Heath, and many others.

III. THE FIRST MAJOR TOURNAMENTS

As women's soccer grew in terms of participation and popularity, women began to lobby for their own tournaments and create national teams. The U.S. team was hastily formed from a group of top collegiate players in 1985 for a tournament in Italy called the Mundialito, or "little World Cup" in Spanish. It featured just four teams: Italy, England, Denmark, and the United States. The American women wore old men's uniforms and even had to sew the letters *USA* on themselves! Can you imagine representing your country on an international stage and needing to stitch your own uniform?

Few of the players knew what it meant to be on a national team. Their coach, Mike Ryan, who coached club teams in Washington and had selected the group, made them sing the national anthem to fill them with patriotic pride.

That first American team played four games in August of 1985, going 0–1–3 and finishing in last place. Nineteen-year-old Michelle Akers, who scored two of the team's three goals, was the lone bright spot in a slew of disappointing matches. They didn't play again until the summer of 1986, again at the Mundialito in Italy, which had now expanded to six teams—Italy, Japan, Mexico, China, Brazil, and the United States. By that time, UNC coach Anson Dorrance had taken over the coaching duties. Clearly the Americans had improved over the course of a year, and this time they won their first three games and advanced to the finals, where they lost to Italy. By 1987, the team had an eleven-game schedule, over the course of three tournaments.

These were the first baby steps.

In 1988, it was time to take larger strides. A prototype of the World Cup, known as the FIFA Women's Invitation Tournament or the International Women's Football Tournament, was held in China, to test if the idea would work. Twelve teams participated from around the world, and in an all-Scandinavian final, Norway beat Sweden, 1–0.

The event brought in great crowds and the competition was fierce, which led the governing body of soccer, FIFA, to deem the concept successful. In November 1991 the first Women's World Cup was held in Guangzhou, China.

China was selected for a couple of reasons. First, the country was trying to win a bid to host the Olympics, and officials were eager to show that the Chinese could host a successful event and sell tickets. Also, at the time, China was still closed off enough from the rest of the world that the event wouldn't attract too much attention. Oddly, that was what FIFA wanted, since the organization was still not fully committed to women's soccer. This was still a small test, which, if successful, could lead to a bigger display.

FIFA didn't even want to call the women's tournament a "World Cup." It wanted to save that special title just for the men's game. So it came up with the ridiculous title of 1st FIFA World Championship for Women's Football for the M&M's Cup. The sponsor was Mars, the maker of M&M's. The games were only eighty minutes, instead of ninety, causing U.S. captain April Heinrichs to joke, "They were afraid our ovaries were going to fall out if we played ninety."

The U.S. team included many of the stars who would go on to become household names a decade later: Mia Hamm, Michelle Akers, Julie Foudy, Brandi Chastain, and Kristine Lilly. The Americans cooked their own food in their hotel and were still wearing boys' uniforms. But they had become a real team, with skill and grit. In China they won all of their games and defeated Norway 2–1 in the final. The games had good attendance, including 65,000 for the final.

But when the team arrived home, the players realized that no one in the United States knew anything about the World Cup. Three people met them at the airport.

"It was such a big deal in China that we thought, 'Oh my God, this will totally change how people view soccer in the States,'" Julie Foudy said.

But it didn't. There was still a lot of work to do.

The U.S. women would play again in the 1995 World Cup in Sweden. By that time, the brand name M&M's had been dropped. The tournament was held in the summer, the games were ninety minutes long, the Scandinavian press paid attention, and it felt more like a proper World Cup. The U.S. team made it to the final before losing 1–0 to Norway. The Americans were bitterly disappointed and the event didn't do much to make the people back home more aware of women's soccer.

But they would get another chance, just a year later. The 1995 World Cup served as the qualifier to the first Olympic women's soccer tournament, which was to be held in the United States in 1996. The Olympics were in Atlanta, but the soccer tournament was held in nearby cities. It was a chance for the U.S. team to grow its game at home.

They did that, drawing crowds of 43,525 at the

Orange Bowl in Miami, 64,196 for a semifinal in Athens, Georgia, and 76,489 for the gold medal game in the same venue. The crowd for the final set a then–world record for attendance at a women's sporting event. Those numbers stunned onlookers and organizers and helped build momentum for the 1999 World Cup, which would put the national team on the sports map forever.

IV. PROFESSIONAL LEAGUES

As women's soccer grew in popularity, so did the push for a professional league in the United States. The desire wasn't just that women players wanted to be able to earn a living playing their sport, like their male counterparts. Leagues were also deemed necessary to continue to improve the sport. Once players were out of college, they had nowhere to play except the national team. But national teams only played sporadically and only had room for the most elite players. How could the sport grow without a league that would help develop players?

The success of the 1999 Women's World Cup gave birth to the Women's United Soccer Association (WUSA). The stars from the 1999 team, and many of the top players around the world, came to play in the league, which was founded in 2000. But having the familiar faces divided among several different teams didn't have the same impact or attraction to fans as the cohesive national team, and interest waned. Plus, the league was built on an unsustainable financial model, with the assumption that television ratings, crowds, and corporate sponsorships would continue to grow. Instead they decreased, the league incurred debt, and after three years—on the eve of the 2003 World Cup— the WUSA shut down operation. It was a huge blow to the players who had built the game.

Some players went overseas to play in leagues in Sweden, Germany, or France. Others played in local semiprofessional leagues.

Another attempt at a league—Women's Professional Soccer (WPS)—was launched in 2009. This league was built more on a grassroots approach, rather than the national structure that doomed the WUSA. Though expectations were modest, the league still struggled to gain a foothold with fans. In addition, it suffered when one of its owners sued the league, diverting resources. That league also only lasted three years, shutting down in 2012.

A third attempt at a professional league began in 2013. The National Women's Soccer League (NWSL) has a different model than the previous leagues. It is administered by the U.S. Soccer Federation. Salaries are low and the league is relying on live-streaming its games online rather than television contracts. The hope is that the league will continue to grow.

Early on, two of the NWSL teams partnered with teams in their cities from the more popular men's league, Major League Soccer. That may be a successful model going forward. In Europe and in other places in the world, successful and established men's soccer clubs partner with women's teams, which has allowed the women's professional league to grow based on a solid foundation.

Around the world, other professional leagues are flourishing. The top female players are finding places to play, even if they come from countries with soccer federations that ignore their women's team unless there is a big event like the Olympics or World Cup.

Women are crisscrossing the globe to play soccer. In 2017, Brazilian star Marta came to the United States to play in Orlando. American stars Carli Lloyd and Alex Morgan went across the Atlantic—to England and

France, respectively—to find new soccer challenges.

It is unrealistic to expect the women's league to become as popular as men's soccer leagues or other men's sports any time soon. The history of professional sports is one of gradual growth, and the men's sports have a more than hundred-year head start on women's leagues. But creating leagues is a major step forward, as they're important for the continued development of players and the growth of the game.

For years, women's soccer was banned, ignored, and belittled. But women refused to give in to the limitations society tried to place on them and continued to play the game.

And they're never going to stop.

TOP TEN GOAL SCORERS IN WOMEN'S INTERNATIONAL SOCCER HISTORY

10. **(TIE) MICHELLE AKERS**, USA, 1985–2000, 155 international caps: 105 goals

10. **(TIE) CAROLINA MORACE**, Italy, 1978–1997, 153 international caps: 105 goals

9. **SUN WEN**, China, 1990–2006, 152 international caps: 106 goals

8. **ELISABETTA VIGNOTTO**, Italy, 1970–1989, 110 international caps: 107 goals

7. **PATRIZIA PANICO***, Italy, 1996–present, 204 international caps: 110 goals

6. **JULIE FLEETING**, Scotland, 1996–2011, 120 international caps: 116 goals

5. **BIRGIT PRINZ**, Germany, 1994–2011, 214 international caps: 128 goals

4. **KRISTINE LILLY**, USA, 1987–2010, 354 international caps: 130 goals

3. **MIA HAMM**, USA, 1987–2004, 276 international caps: 158 goals

2. **CHRISTINE SINCLAIR***, Canada, 2000–present, 253 international caps: 168 goals
1. **ABBY WAMBACH**, USA, 2001–2015, 256 international caps: 184 goals

current player

►►► **SECOND HALF**

THE INTERNATIONAL STARTING 11

MARTA

*There's still the prejudice of thinking women are
the weaker sex or that they weren't born to play
sports. I think people need to stop that and give
us credit.*

—Marta

I f you took a vote of who is the greatest women's
soccer player of all time, that vote would probably
be close to unanimous.

Her name is Marta. Or as her Brazilian fans call
her, "*Pelé con faldas.*" That's Portuguese for "Pelé with
skirts," which is considered a compliment even if Marta
wears shorts and cleats—not skirts—to practice her
talent.

Like Pelé, considered the greatest man to ever play
the game, Marta is Brazilian. And she goes by one
name, as do almost all extremely famous Brazilian
athletes, including Pelé.

Unfortunately, unlike Pelé, Marta has never been

able to win a World Cup championship in her prime, nor has she won an Olympic gold medal. However, those shortcomings were due more to the failure of the system she played in, rather than related to her own breathtaking talents.

Marta Vieira da Silva was born on February 19, 1986, in Alagoas, in the eastern part of Brazil. Soccer is such an important sport in Brazil that almost every child grows up playing barefoot on the streets. Marta was no different, though as a girl she was sometimes shunned by boys who resented her skills. Even her own brothers and father disapproved.

"Some boys accepted me, some didn't," she said. "And my family had comments made to them. Brazil is still a very macho society and sports are mainly for boys, so people would say to them, 'What is this girl doing? Why is she always out there in the soccer games with the boys?'"

When Marta was fourteen, friends who had moved to Rio de Janeiro told her that one of the big clubs, Vasco da Gama, was having tryouts for a women's team. Marta made the three-day bus trip to get to Rio, where she put on cleats for the first time. The coach of the team was named Helena Pacheco, who quickly recognized that Marta was a diamond in the rough. But the club struggled because of a lack of funds, and it folded. By the time she was eighteen, in 2004, Marta had already been called up by the Brazilian national team and played in the 2003 World Cup as a seventeen-year-old. A coach from Sweden saw her compete there and convinced Marta to move away from the steamy heat of Rio to the chill of Sweden to play soccer for Umeå IK, near the Arctic Circle.

Though Marta's talents had yet to be fully unleashed, she was a tantalizing prospect. She was a compact (five-foot-four), lightning-quick, skilled player who seemed to keep the ball connected to her foot by an invisible string.

In the 2004 Olympics, in Athens, the world got its first real look at Marta. Just eighteen, she scored three goals in her team's first four games, helping her team reach the finals against the United States. The U.S. team beat Brazil 2–1, but it took until the 112th minute when Abby Wambach scored the game-winner. It was the furthest Brazil had ever gotten in a major tournament, and the silver medal performance signaled that, with Marta at forward, Brazil was a new power.

But despite her talent, and the team's growing

success, Marta and her teammates constantly had to fight for themselves and battle against sexism. As in many other parts of the world, Brazil did not encourage women's soccer, even as the men's game was built into a world power and the sport was celebrated throughout the country. The measures the country took to maintain this unequal status quo were so extreme that there was a law from 1941 to 1979 to prevent girls from playing soccer, even in school.

Yet because Brazil is extremely proud of its soccer heritage, regardless of this unfair and negative perception of girls playing sports, there is still tremendous pressure on its women's team to perform. It seems almost contradictory. The country has had a national team since 1986, but it has suffered from lack of funding and continuity. Women's soccer players have been treated as second-class citizens. Yet when you become a member of the national team, you are expected to win because you are Brazilian. It's a difficult line to walk.

Although Brazil has a rich soccer tradition, Marta had to leave her country to truly develop her skills. She always had speed, but she became more adept at finding the open space and beating defenders. She played in Sweden for five seasons, leading her team to league titles four times and to the UEFA championship once. She led the league in scoring three times in five years.

In the 2007 World Cup, in a semifinal game against the United States, Marta put on an exciting spectacle that opened eyes around the world. Her second goal, the fourth of the game, is considered one of the great goals in World Cup history. And because it came against the popular American team, it was noticed by fans and experts around the world.

Marta trapped the ball above the left side of the box, flicked the ball past the defender to herself, dribbled around another defender, and shot into the corner.

"It was my most beautiful goal," Marta said.

It was a dazzling one-woman display. Marta's two goals helped her Brazilian team knock out the United States in the semifinals. After such an incredible performance, it seemed as though Brazil was destined to win a championship. But in the finals, they lost to Germany.

In the 2008 Olympics, the United States faced Brazil in the gold medal game. Marta again was breathtaking in her speed and skill, but several of her shots were saved by U.S. goalkeeper Hope Solo, and once again the Brazilians were runners-up.

By then, Marta was on an unprecedented run, winning the FIFA women's player of the year award in five consecutive years. She was clearly the best player in the world, but she didn't have the team around her or the full support of her federation to get onto the top podium.

This streak of never quite making it to the top continued over the next few years. In 2011, her team was ousted again by the United States, this time in the quarterfinals. The game was one of the thrillers in World Cup history, with the U.S. team tying it up in the 122nd minute and then winning on penalty kicks. In the London Olympics, Brazil lost in the quarterfinals to reigning World Cup champion Japan.

As Marta got older, there were no Brazilian players coming up who were talented enough to make a major impact. And Brazil's results began to decline. The team was ousted in the first knockout round of the Canada World Cup in 2015.

Most heartbreaking for Marta was the Rio Olympics, a moment that the women's soccer players of Brazil hoped would finally win them the long-sought support of their country. The women's team had not played many times at home in Brazil and had only played in Maracanã, the most fabled stadium in South America, once before. This was their chance to galvanize their country.

Despite dazzling play in group play, when Brazil crushed China and Sweden, and getting through the quarterfinals on penalty kicks, Brazil faltered in the semifinals. Playing against Sweden in Maracanã, in front of 70,000 fans—the largest crowd to ever watch a women's game in Brazil—the Brazilian team was frustrated and unable to score. The team lost on penalty kicks.

To add insult to injury, many of Marta's close friends, women that she had played with or against professionally for years in Sweden, were on the team that eliminated Brazil.

"They praised our team and said they were sorry for taking Brazil out of the final," Marta said after the game. "They wanted to see us playing in the final here in Brazil. But this is football. Someone has to lose."

All the while, as Marta dominated on the international stage, she struggled to find a professional home, as do so many women players. After playing in Sweden, she came to the United States and played in the WPS, and in the off-season, played in Brazil for Santos. In 2012, after the WPS folded, she went back to Sweden to play. She speaks Swedish and became a Swedish citizen just seven months after her newly adopted country had ousted her birth country from the Olympics. She said she will continue to play internationally for Brazil.

In 2017, Marta bounced around yet again and returned to the United States to play for Orlando in the NWSL.

Still, on the international stage, Marta reigns supreme. She holds the record for the most goals scored in Women's World Cup history. She also has been an outspoken and ardent ambassador for the women's game, helping to promote it in South America and other countries.

Her hope is that the next "best player in the women's game" won't have to fight the battles that she has faced. Whenever she arrives on the scene, that is. Until that day, Marta stands alone as the greatest of all time.

STATISTICS:

Position: forward

World Cup runner-up (2007)

Two-time Olympic silver medalist (2004, 2008)

101 appearances for the Brazilian national team

105 goals

HOMARE SAWA

Don't just dream your dreams—make
them come true.

—Homare Sawa

One of the most powerful and beautiful things about sports is its ability to unite and inspire a country. And no example of that has been more dramatic than the way Japan's Homare Sawa and her teammates impacted their country in 2011.

In March 2011, a devastating earthquake and tsunami ravaged parts of Japan. The death and destruction was shocking: an estimated 16,000 people were killed and more than 230,000 people were displaced from their homes. A large nuclear power plant was severely damaged and leaked radiation into the surrounding communities and water supplies, causing further harm that would affect Japan for years to come.

With that national tragedy as a backdrop, the Japanese women's soccer team arrived at the World Cup in Germany in June 2011. The team, nicknamed Nadeshiko—after a pink flower native to Japan—was captained by Homare. At each match, she and her teammates unfurled a large banner on the field, thanking the world for its support of their country. The tragedy was never far from their minds and hearts.

"As players, there is nothing much we can do for Japan, but we want do to as well as we can to help our country," Homare said.

The Japanese team certainly did that, transfixing the entire country back home and the rest of the world. The small and underestimated team knocked off the giants of the sport on its way to a World Cup championship.

Homare was born in Tokyo in 1978 and started playing soccer at age six with her brother. She began playing professionally in Japan's L League when she was just twelve years old. By the time she made her first appearance for the Japanese national team in 1993, when she was fifteen, she was already well known in her country. She quickly proved that she deserved her reputation, scoring four goals in her first national team game.

She was the best player in Japan for many years, leading her team to six World Cups, from the 1995 tournament in Sweden through the 2015 tournament in Canada. That longevity gave her the distinction of being one of just two athletes of either sex (the other is Brazil's Formiga) to play in six World Cups. Homare also represented Japan in four Olympics: 1996, 2004, 2008, and 2012 in London, where Japan won the silver medal.

Homare, who was called the "Mia Hamm of Japan," played professionally for many years, including in the WUSA in Atlanta. She later played in the NWSL for Washington. Most of her club career was spent in Japan with the team NTV Beleza.

But it was in Germany in 2011 where Homare, then thirty-two, transcended her status as a sports celebrity and became a national icon.

With her trademark waist-length ponytail swinging behind her, she started her World Cup by sending a message—loud and clear. She scored three goals—a hat trick—against Mexico in group play. That victory helped her team into the second round. Fueled by watching pregame pictures of the devastation in their homeland, the Japanese team knocked off host Germany in the quarterfinals, a shocking upset. Then Homare scored a goal in Japan's 3–1 semifinal victory over Sweden, setting up a final against the heavily favored United States.

The U.S. team had never lost to Japan, going into the final with a 22–0–3 record against their opponent. The Americans had already beaten the Japanese team three times earlier in 2011. But Japan, inspired by their country's emotions, were now playing at a different level. Thanks in large part to Homare's artistry and skill, Japan dazzled opponents with their passes and ball possession.

"She's a great leader," U.S. captain Christie Rampone said before the final. "Their team gets their pulse through her. We have to shut her down."

But they were unable to—in a thrilling match that transfixed fans in Japan and around the world. After regulation ended in a 1–1 tie, the United States took the lead in the first overtime period. Japan's dream of victory seemed to be slipping away as time dwindled down. But Homare was unfazed. In the 117th minute, she stepped up big-time, redirecting a corner kick into the net to tie the game! The match went to penalty kicks and Japan prevailed, 3–1.

When they won, fans in Tokyo rushed out into the dawn to celebrate in the streets.

Homare was awarded the Golden Boot as the MVP of the tournament. She also was named the top player of the year by FIFA.

Twelve months later, she led her team to a rematch with the Americans in the gold medal game of the London Olympics. Japan had knocked off Brazil and France on its way to the final but couldn't overcome the Americans a second time, losing 2–1.

Homare retired after the 2012 Olympics but returned to the game in 2014 at age thirty-five, helping Japan claim the winning trophy in the Asian Games. In the lead-up to the 2015 World Cup, Homare battled a knee injury and at one point was dropped from the team. She was such a star that her absence made headlines in her country. But she was back in the starting lineup for the World Cup in Canada, with her coach saying that her addition made the team "more powerful."

There was pressure on Japan to repeat as champions.

"Other teams look at us differently now," Homare said.

Japan won all of its games in the group stage and was 6–0 as it headed into the final, once again facing the American team. But this time Japan was overwhelmed from the start, as the United States poured in four goals in the first sixteen minutes on its way to a 5–2 victory.

A few months later, Homare announced her retirement at age thirty-seven. By that time she had married a fellow soccer player. In January 2017 the couple welcomed their first baby, a daughter.

Homare plans to stay involved in soccer and somehow take part in the 2020 Tokyo Olympics, understanding the importance and pride of representing one's country. That is when the beloved soccer team that inspired a country in one of its darkest moments will be celebrated at home.

STATISTICS:

Position: midfielder
World Cup champion (2011), runner-up (2015)
204 appearances for the Japanese national team
83 goals

KELLY SMITH

I started at age 8 playing on local boys'
teams . . . I've gathered a treasure trove
of lessons and memories.

—Kelly Smith

occer—or as most of the rest of the world calls it,
football—was invented in England. And many
English soccer fans have been known to express
"traditional attitudes" about the sport. Which means
they were very slow to embrace women's soccer. In
fact, the sport was banned as "unsuitable" for women
by the FA, a ban that stood for fifty years, until 1971.

But thanks to Kelly Smith, attitudes about women's
soccer started to change in England.

Kelly is considered the most important English
female player in history. And she had to fight a lot of
battles to get that recognition.

Kelly was born in 1978 and grew up in Watford.

She played for a local boys' team, but when she was seven, she had to quit even though she was the team's top goal scorer. That's because the parents of the opposing teams objected to playing against her.

"It was a problem for them to see a girl like me dominating a game featuring their sons," Kelly said.

Her father formed a girls' team, which he coached, and Kelly was soon recognized as a top prospect. When she was eighteen, she began playing with Arsenal Ladies, an amateur women's team affiliated with the famous Arsenal men's club.

By that time, she was already a member of the English national team, debuting in 1995 at age seventeen. She had been unable to accept an invitation to join the team for the 1995 World Cup because she had been taking her secondary school exams at the time. England lost in the quarterfinals of that 1995 tournament and, unfortunately for Kelly, the country did not make it back to another World Cup until 2007.

Like some other successful international players, Kelly came to the United States to improve her game at the collegiate level. Other countries don't have the established sports programs that American universities do, and Kelly found a spot where she could thrive at Seton Hall in New Jersey. In three years at Seton Hall, from 1997 to 1999, she set scoring records for both the school and the conference and was one of the top players in the country.

After college, citing the poor state of women's soccer in her native country, she opted to stay in the United States.

"Women's football in England is a joke," she said at the time.

She was selected by the Philadelphia Charge in the 2001 WUSA draft. But in 2002 she tore the ACL in her right knee, which marked the beginning of a long string of injuries to come. Those included tearing her other ACL and breaking her leg. Depressed by the long stints of rehabilitation, Kelly developed a serious drinking problem. She sought help when she returned to England and checked herself into a rehabilitation clinic, where she was successfully treated.

Women's soccer was beginning to gain some momentum in England at the time and Kelly returned to Arsenal, which was semiprofessional by then. With Kelly as its centerpiece, Arsenal dominated women's soccer in England. Over her years with Arsenal, she won six titles, five FA Cups, and the Champions League.

Yet England still struggled on the international stage. While most of the all-time greats played in many World Cups throughout their careers, Kelly had to wait a long time before her first chance came along.

At the 2007 World Cup in China, Kelly's first, she scored two goals against Japan in the second half, and, having waited so long for the opportunity, celebrated by taking off her cleats and kissing them. But the celebration made her coach, Hope Powell, angry, and she prohibited the behavior. Her coach may not have liked it, but the action got a lot of notice back home and inspired a lot of little girls who played soccer. England was knocked out by the United States in the quarterfinals, but Kelly had made a lasting impression in spite of the disappointing finish.

In 2011 in Germany, England was again knocked out in the World Cup quarterfinals. The team's best showing was in 2015, when it finished a surprising third, beating Germany in the third-place game. But Kelly missed the tournament, once again hampered by injury. She tore ankle ligaments early in 2015 and spent the World Cup working as a television broadcaster.

Kelly had even fewer chances to make an impact

in the Olympics. In fact, she had just one. But it was perhaps the biggest moment of her career, which came when London hosted the 2012 Olympics. She was on team Great Britain, which received an automatic berth as host. Great Britain created a women's team specifically for the Olympics; before that, England, Wales, Northern Ireland, and Scotland had competed as separate teams. It was the only time Great Britain entered a women's team in the Olympics.

The competition was at first dismissed by the British media, which made jokes about female footballers. Such attitudes were surprising to visitors from other countries where women's soccer had been popular for many years. But those jokes subsided when the public enthusiasm for the game became obvious. Thousands of fans packed the stadiums— some of soccer's most iconic structures—to see the women play.

Kelly and her team played Brazil at Wembley Stadium, and 70,584 fans filled the stadium to see England's 1–0 victory.

"We got a tremendous amount of exposure," said Kelly, whose team lost the next match, to Canada. "It was a once-in-a-lifetime opportunity. To play in front of record crowds, to get people to come out and support women's football was fantastic."

Because of the complicated nature of putting together a Great Britain team, there was no follow-up at the Rio Olympics. But the image of the roaring home crowd in 2011 was forever stamped in Kelly's mind.

Kelly retired in the beginning of 2017, at age thirty-eight, as England's record holder for the most goals scored in a career, forty-six. She joined Arsenal as an assistant coach and also announced that she and her wife, DeAnna, were expecting a baby.

By the time her playing career ended, there was a Women's Super League in England, with many teams affiliated with the powerful, established men's clubs. The league is run by the same Football Association that once had banned the sport.

The world of women's football had evolved, and Kelly was instrumental in bringing about change.

"I was at the bottom, and I have seen it grow to what it is now," Kelly said. "If any recognition came my way, then that was great because it helped the game grow."

STATISTICS:

Position: forward

117 appearances for England's national team

4 appearances for Great Britain

46 goals

CHRISTINE SINCLAIR

*For me, I watched the women's 1999 World
Cup and that changed my life . . . I knew
what I wanted to do, so hopefully some of
the young kids in the stands throughout
the World Cup feel the same way and now
have a dream and a passion to represent
[their countries]. And yeah, there's a
responsibility to that, but I've been waiting
my whole career for this opportunity.*

—Christine Sinclair

If you were to poll a group of people and ask who
has the second most goals in the history of international women's soccer—right behind scoring leader
Abby Wambach—you would probably hear a variety
of answers, including "Mia Hamm" and "Marta."

Those answers would be wrong. Because that
lofty position belongs to Christine Sinclair of Canada.

Christine is the best player in the world that a lot
of people don't know about. That might be because

she plays for Canada, a country that for a long time had not achieved much success in the soccer world.

But Christine helped change that. At one point, American goalkeeper Hope Solo, who played against Christine for years both in college and in international matches, called her "the best player in the world."

Christine was born in British Columbia in 1983. She started playing soccer in her home town of Burnaby at age four—for the Burna Bees. Both of her parents and her older brother played soccer, and two of her uncles played in Portland for the North American Soccer League in the late 1970s and early 1980s.

Soccer "was just something our family did," said Christine, who actually stopped by a soccer field on her way home from the hospital, just hours after being born! Her mother coached the team and wanted to show off her new baby.

Christine also played baseball. She played second base and wore No. 12 in honor of her favorite player, Roberto Alomar, who was the second baseman for the Toronto Blue Jays. She kept that number on the soccer field.

And as she improved on the field and got older, it became clear that Christine had a great shot at becoming a pro soccer player. In 1999—by then a youth star in British Columbia—Christine headed south to Portland to attend a match at the 1999 Women's World Cup. Witnessing the incredible athleticism on display, she became determined to play for her national team. At that point, Canada had not done very much in the world of soccer, never having made it out of group play in two World Cups in 1995 and 1999 and failing to qualify for the Olympics.

Christine wouldn't have to wait very long for an opportunity to arise. A few months later, in 2000, she made her national team debut at just sixteen at the Algarve Cup. Full of nerves, she found it awkward to play with such older women. But you couldn't tell that from her performance on the field—she finished with three goals, the most of any player in the tournament. It marked a turning point as she helped to start to change the mentality of Canada's team, which was accustomed to being drubbed by other teams, including their American neighbors.

In the early 2000s, Christine was becoming a better and better player. She attended the University of Portland, which had a strong history of women's soccer, and led the Pilots to two national championships.

She won the Hermann Trophy—as the top collegiate player—in consecutive seasons and set a single-season Division 1 scoring record with thirty-nine goals in the 2005 season. She also earned a degree in life science.

Her scoring ability wasn't just being showcased in college. In 2002, she scored seven goals in the 2002 Gold Cup and ten at the U-19 World Cup, where Canada finished second. Christine took a redshirt season at Portland, meaning she sat out a year of college, in order to play for Canada in the 2003 World Cup, fulfilling that dream she'd formed four years earlier. There, she scored three goals, including her team's first goal of the tournament against eventual champion Germany, and helped Canada to a fourth-place finish. Canada lost to Sweden in a semifinal and to the United States in the third-place match, but advancing to the semifinals was a pivotal moment for Canada.

With Christine on the roster, Canada played in the 2007 and 2011 World Cups, but without much of a supporting cast around their leader, the team didn't make it out of group stage in either tournament. It was the 2012 London Olympics where Christine and Canada made their biggest statement.

Motivated in part by the fact that Canada would

host the next big event—the 2015 World Cup—Christine and her teammates played with determination. They advanced out of group play and knocked off host England in the quarterfinal, setting up a semifinal match with the United States, the team Canada considered its primary rival and "big sister."

In one of the great games in Olympic history—some have dubbed it "the greatest game ever"—played at historic Old Trafford in Manchester, England, Christine was a superstar. She scored three goals and with each goal, she kept her team one step ahead of the heavily favored Americans.

Christine scored the first goal of the game in the 22nd minute. After the Americans tied it, Christine was on the attack again.

In the 67th minute she raised her hand in front of the goal to signal to her teammate that she was open, rose up over her opponent to get her head on the ball, and knocked it in past her old collegiate rival Hope Solo. Canada was up 2–1.

The U.S. team came back to tie once again, but in the 73rd minute, Christine put in a corner kick for her third goal. An Olympic hat trick! She raised her arms in triumph.

But there was still too much time left for the Americans.

On a controversial play, the referee awarded the U.S. team an indirect free kick because she ruled that the Canadian goalkeeper was wasting time—a rare call. On the ensuing play, the official called a handball on Canada, leading to a penalty kick. Abby Wambach converted it, tying the game and sending it into extra time. In the 122nd minute—extra overtime—Alex Morgan headed the ball in for the game-winner.

It was a crushing loss. Naturally, Christine was upset with the outcome—in particular the official's heavy influence in deciding the game—and didn't hold back in telling the public know how she truly felt.

"We feel cheated," she said afterward. "We feel like we didn't lose, we feel like it was taken from us. It's a shame in a game like that, that was so important, the ref decided the result before it started."

But in the privacy of the dressing room, with her teammates, Christine didn't wallow in the loss. Instead she told her team, "We have a bronze medal to win." And they did, beating France 1–0, which at the time was the best finish by Canada at a major tournament. Christine was chosen by her Olympic teammates to carry her country's flag in the closing ceremonies.

Three years later, when Canada hosted the Women's World Cup, Christine was the face of the event. She was even on a postage stamp! The usually shy and humble player was a huge celebrity in her country and was the focus of attention. After the finish in London, there were high expectations, but Canada lost 2–1 to England in the quarterfinals. Christine scored the only goal and was in tears after the loss, feeling she had let her country down.

The next year, at the Rio Olympics, it was Christine's team that broke the heart of the hosts. Canada again advanced to the bronze medal game, having already beaten a strong French team and eventual champion Germany in the group stage. In the bronze medal match, Canada beat host Brazil 2–1. It was Christine's goal in the 52nd minute—she trapped a pass in front of Brazil's goal with her left foot and sent it into the right corner with her right—that was the difference in the game. It was the 165th goal of her career.

With the victory, Canada moved up to fourth in the world in the FIFA rankings. That's an accomplishment few could have imagined was possible back when Christine started playing for the national squad. She had changed not only the mentality but the reality for Team Canada.

"I think it's night and day," she said. "The mentality of the team now is we're heading into every game to win."

Despite a lengthy career, Christine—who also had a successful professional career with the Portland Thorns of the NWSL—said she wasn't ready to retire.

"I have loftier goals so I'm not done yet," she said. "I still have a passion to improve. A passion to help my team."

The best player that many have never heard of is still making noise.

STATISTICS*:

Position: forward
Two-time Olympic bronze medalist (2012, 2016)
259 appearances for the Canadian national team
168 goals
*current player

SUN WEN

Passersby thought it was strange and unacceptable
to see a girl kicking a ball against a wall. I didn't
care. I played so much my parents had to buy me
new sneakers every month.

—Sun Wen

The rapid growth of women's soccer is usually credited to the rise of women's athletics in the United States due to the passage of Title IX.

But it is worth remembering that the first Women's World Cup was held in China in 1991. It was the momentous event that set women's soccer on the path to becoming a major international sport.

And that initial tournament helped launch Sun Wen, one of the greatest women's soccer players in history and the most important in China's history.

Wen was born in Shanghai in 1973. Her father liked to play soccer for fun and took his young daughter with him so she could watch his games. She started playing the sport around age eight and, like her American counterparts, she played with boys. And she played well. That was around the same time that China started a women's national team, expanding opportunities for female athletes in the country. Like the United States, China did not have a strong men's soccer tradition, so there was plenty of room for the women's game to grow.

Yet girls, like Wen, still faced disapproval for playing. Wen remembers people staring at her when she kicked the ball against the wall, thinking—as Wen recalled—"it was unacceptable to see a girl kicking a ball." Because China had a strict one-child policy in an attempt to control its population size, parents had a heightened concern about rough sports that could injure their beloved child. Wen's own mother was not in favor of her playing, preferring that she concentrate on her studies.

Wen played for her school, which won a district championship, and she scored the most goals. When she was thirteen, her father took her to a local sports school for a tryout. That was how China developed its national athletes, through academies designed to help the country's Olympic programs succeed. The schools were very strict, almost like military camp. Though Wen had less experience than the competition, she was chosen by the academy. And at age sixteen, Wen was selected to play for the national team.

China was eager to have a strong team, as it had been selected to host the first Women's World Cup in 1991—the result of having hosted an early version of the tournament in 1988. FIFA, the organization that runs international soccer, was reluctant to use the term *World Cup* for a women's tournament, so the 1991 tournament was called the 1st FIFA World Championship for Women's Football for the M&M's Cup and was sponsored by the candy company Mars.

Wen was only eighteen during the World Cup and had played in just three international matches. The Chinese women were the favorites to win the tournament. There was tremendous pressure on the team.

Wen, a forward, started all four games that China played, scoring in a tie game against Denmark. China advanced to the second round in that tournament but didn't meet expectations, losing to Sweden in the quarterfinals. The team's coach became despondent after the defeat, and the team lost funding and disbanded for almost a year.

Four years later, Wen was the star of the much-improved Chinese team. Her speed allowed her to get behind defenses, and her diminutive size allowed her to get lost by defenders. Her greatest attribute may have been her soccer IQ—she had a reputation for being a very smart player. She could score with either foot and was a master at ball control. In 1995, her team made it to the semifinals of the World Cup in Sweden, losing 1–0 to Germany. During the tournament, Wen added two more goals to her World Cup total.

In 1996, for the first time, women's soccer was an event at the Olympics, which took place in Atlanta that year. The top eight teams from the 1995 World Cup were selected to compete, China among them. It was a historic moment in the history of the sport.

That first Olympics for women's soccer also marked the rise of a Chinese team that was out to prove something to the world. China made it to the gold medal game of the Olympics, where it faced off against the impressive U.S. team. After the Americans scored a goal early, Wen tied the match in the 32nd minute, but China ultimately fell to the U.S. team and finished with the silver medal. That match set up the epic showdown that was to come in 1999.

In 1999, while the U.S. team was drawing enormous crowds and huge excitement, on the other side of the bracket, Wen was dominating. Her team had a brutal schedule for the World Cup, having to fly back and forth across the United States four times during the tournament. But the team found a large and enthusiastic fan base among Chinese Americans, who brought the team food and made them feel welcome.

Wen had become very famous in China. She wrote poetry that appeared in the newspapers. Chinese reporters tracked everything she did during the 1999 World Cup—which was quite a lot.

The captain of the team, Wen scored seven goals, including a hat trick against Ghana, and led China to the finals, where they lost 1–0 to the Americans in an epic match that was decided on penalty kicks. Sun Wen made her kick, but her team lost. After the game, she and Mia Hamm exchanged jerseys and Hamm told Wen, "You were the best player in the World Cup." Wen, indeed, did win the Golden Ball as the tournament's MVP, as well as the Golden Boot for highest scorer.

"The U.S. was more lucky," Wen said after the game. "The reason they won the game is because the support of women's soccer is so great in the United States."

The team's performance led to a boom in popularity for the sport in China immediately following the 1999 World Cup. Women's leagues could now outdraw men's leagues, and financial support increased as well.

Yet that was the pinnacle of China's performance. In the 2000 Olympics, China didn't make it out of the group stage. And in the 2003 World Cup, which was originally supposed to take place in China but had to be moved to the United States, China lost in the quarterfinals.

Wen came to the United States and played for the Atlanta Beat in the WUSA in 2001 and 2002, but she struggled with injuries. She retired from the club in early 2003 in order to rest her body and prepare for that year's World Cup. She retired for good in 2006.

After her retirement she became the director of technical and youth associations for a soccer club in Shanghai. She had seen China surpassed by Japan as the top country in Asia. But Wen was working to help recruit young women to soccer to carry on her legacy, one of the brightest in the game.

STATISTICS:

Position: forward

World Cup runner-up (1999)

Olympic silver medalist (1996)

152 appearances for the Chinese national team

106 goals

BIRGIT PRINZ

Why stop? It's always good for players'
confidence when they score.

—Birgit Prinz

Germany's Birgit Prinz probably did more for the acceptance of women by the international soccer world than any other player.

While American players became stars in their own right, they were viewed by the rest of the world as not particularly significant, because they weren't from a soccer powerhouse nation like Brazil or Italy. Despite the national team's success, the United States just wasn't particularly important in the larger world of soccer since American fans have only recently started taking an interest in the sport.

But in Germany, soccer was a *big deal*. Germany is a soccer powerhouse, with the men's team having won a total of four World Cups. So when women's soccer began to grow, the stage was set for a great female player to come along and become a national hero. Sure enough, Birgit became a force on her country's women's national team soon after joining the squad in 1994.

Before long, Birgit became known as the best women's soccer player in Europe.

Birgit was born in Frankfurt in 1977 and was a good all-around athlete, swimming and competing in track-and-field. She began playing in youth soccer leagues, where her father was a coach. Germany had a history of established leagues for girls and by 1990 had a semiprofessional women's league. She played for two clubs and then moved up to FSV Frankfurt in 1993. With Frankfurt, she won two Bundesliga titles and two German Cup championships and was the league's top scorer twice. In 1998, she moved to rival FFC Frankfurt, where she had even greater success, winning six Bundesliga titles and eight German Cups.

Birgit, a tall, powerful forward, was a nightmare for defenders. She was taller than most of the opposition and had a higher fitness level. Her speed and power, as well as her accuracy in front of the goal, soon made her the top female player in all of Europe. In her international debut for the German national team in 1994, she blasted the game-winning goal against Canada in the 89th minute, a calling card for what was to come.

Her Frankfurt coach, Siegfried Dietrich, said Birgit was "the most complete player in the world, a powerful representative of German women's football."

In her first World Cup in 1995, at just seventeen, she helped Germany advance to the final, becoming the youngest player ever to appear in a World Cup final, though the team lost to Norway. In the 1999 World Cup, Birgit added another goal to her career total, but she hadn't yet emerged as the superstar she would soon become, and Germany lost to the Americans in the quarterfinals.

Over the next few years, Birgit truly entered her prime, showcasing her talents on the international stage. Germany won five European Championships with Birgit leading the way. But its most significant achievement was winning back-to-back World Cup titles. In 2003, Germany knocked out the reigning world champion Americans in the semifinal. Birgit scored in the 3–0 shutout. Then her team beat Sweden in the final and Birgit was honored as the top player in the tournament, leading all scorers with seven goals. She won both the Golden Ball and Golden Boot trophies.

The tournament was a breakthrough for women's soccer in Germany. The final was watched by 10.5 million viewers on German television, and thousands turned out to welcome the team home to Frankfurt. Birgit's popularity was instrumental in the enthusiasm. With the victory, Germany became the first and only country in the world to have claimed the World Cup in both men's and women's soccer.

In the 2007 World Cup in China, Germany was again the dominant team. In the final against Brazil, Birgit scored perhaps the biggest goal of her career, in the 52nd minute. She received a pass from a teammate in front of the goal and slotted the ball in for the first score of the game. Germany went on to win the game and defend its title.

A month later, and a year after the triumphant hosting of the men's World Cup, Germany was awarded the right to host the 2011 Women's World Cup. The women's back-to-back championships were instrumental in the successful bid, and Prinz was an enthusiastic spokeswoman for the proposal, helping to lobby support.

During this run of victories, Birgit was named the FIFA player of the year for three consecutive years, from 2003 to 2005. In her era, she was as dominating as Marta would be later, though Birgit was a taller player and had a more physically imposing style. She also led her team to the Olympic bronze medal three times, in 2000, 2004, and 2008.

Like many of the best players in the world, she moved to the United States to play in the WUSA in the early 2000s, joining the Carolina Courage. Fresh off another championship with her old team in Frankfurt, she dominated the WUSA competition and led Carolina to the championship, scoring one goal and assisting another in the title game.

Birgit became such a household name that in 2003, she received a surprise request: a men's Serie A team in Italy wanted to recruit her to play for their team. But she declined the offer, afraid it would be perceived only as a publicity stunt.

Birgit enjoyed years of amazing success, but of course, as athletes get older, their skills start to falter. When

Germany hosted the Women's World Cup in 2011, Birgit was thirty-three years old and her ability was on the decline. As reigning two-time champions, Germany was a favorite, but when the team struggled Prinz was blamed. She was under tremendous scrutiny from the German press, with her body language analyzed in the newspapers and calls for her to be removed from the starting lineup. She eventually was benched. It was a difficult situation for a very private person who had only known success.

In the quarterfinal, the hosts were upset by Japan—which would go on to win the World Cup. By failing to finish high enough in the rankings, Germany did not qualify for the 2012 Summer Olympics, a double blow.

After the 2011 World Cup it was clear to Birgit that her career was over. She retired a month later. Germany would have to face its future without its greatest star. At the end of her career, Birgit was ranked first in World Cup goals with fourteen and tied for first in Olympic goals with ten. She was also the most capped player in German history and had scored the most goals ever for the women's national team.

In retirement, she works as a sports psychologist with TSG 1899 Hoffenheim, a team in Germany's

Bundesliga, and also worked with FIFA as a researcher on a project on mental health and sport.

It is fitting that Birgit is working to help players deal with the pressures that come with sports. She can provide her own personal experience, as the woman who helped change perceptions about women's soccer.

STATISTICS:

Position: forward

214 appearances for the German national team

128 goals

NADINE ANGERER

My motto: the older you get the more
relaxed you get.

—Nadine Angerer

Sometimes greatness is hiding in plain sight.

That was the case for Nadine Angerer, who became one of the great goalkeepers the women's game had ever seen. But it took an injury—or two—to let her talent blossom.

Nadine was Germany's backup keeper for many years, making her debut with the national team in 1996. She was born in 1978 and grew up outside Frankfurt. She originally played as a forward, even playing on Germany's under-16 national team as a forward. But after she took over for an injured goalkeeper in a youth tournament, her skills in the net were noticed by her coaches.

She played for a couple of professional teams in Germany, as well as in Sweden and Australia, and rejected an opportunity to come to the United States to play college ball.

By 1996 she had earned a place on the German national team but only played sporadically, warming the bench behind starter Silke Rottenberg. Nadine won European Championships, two Olympic bronze medals, and a Women's World Cup in 2003 while barely getting her uniform dirty.

But in 2007, Rottenberg tore her knee ligament, and Nadine became the starter for the Women's World Cup in China. She was a revelation. Throughout the tournament, she didn't allow a single goal, setting a record for the most consecutive shutout minutes in a World Cup, at 540! She came up *huge* in the final game, blocking a penalty kick by the world's most danger-ous player, Marta of Brazil, as Germany won its second consecutive title.

"I had to prove I deserved it," she said. "Every single match in China was very, very emotional for me right from kickoff. I put an unbelievable amount of pressure on myself."

Nadine became one of the undisputed leaders of

the German team and was named captain after Birgit Prinz retired. Germany's coach Silvia Neid considered her goalkeeper a second coach on the field, calling Nadine her "right hand."

Blocking penalty kicks, a truly difficult feat, became what Nadine was known for: she did it several times in key situations. She saved two penalty kicks in the women's European Championship final in 2013.

"There are not tactics behind it," Nadine said. "It's just intuition. I just try to wait as long as possible and choose a corner."

After the 2013 season, at age thirty-five, Nadine was named the FIFA women's player of the year, becoming the only goalkeeper—male or female—to ever earn FIFA's highest honor.

But her penalty blocking skills failed her in the 2015 World Cup semifinal. Though Germany was the No. 1 ranked team in the world heading into the tournament, they were ousted by the United States. Nadine gave up a crucial penalty kick to Carli Lloyd in the 2–0 defeat.

At the time, she was club teammates with one of the biggest American stars, Alex Morgan. Nadine joined the Portland Thorns of the NWSL in 2014 and fell in love with the city and the enthusiastic fan base. She retired from soccer at age thirty-five, after the 2015 World Cup. She returned to Germany after her retirement to study athletic training, and in 2016 she rejoined the Thorns as the goalkeeper coach.

"I think one of the biggest weak points, especially for a goalkeeper in women's soccer, is they need to be more athletic," she said. "Everything is about athleticism. That's why I did some further education, especially in athletic training."

Now, she will take the skills she mastered throughout her impressive career and pass them on to the next generation of potential greats.

As Nadine understands all too well, you never know when the right opportunity to shine might come along.

STATISTICS:

Position: goalkeeper
Two-time World Cup champion (2003, 2007)
Three-time Olympic bronze medalist (2000, 2004, 2008)
146 appearances for the German national team

LOTTA SCHELIN

*There is always a need to prove to young girls
that it's possible to succeed, that you can do what
you want regardless, and that you shouldn't feel
restricted in any way because of your sex.*

—Lotta Schelin

Women's soccer has a long history in Sweden. Sweden has the oldest and most established women's professional league, which began in 1973 and has attracted some of the top players in the world.

Sweden, like the United States, has competed in every Women's World Cup and made it out of group play in all but one. Sweden has also played in every Olympic women's soccer tournament ever held.

Naturally, over the years, Sweden has produced many good players. But there's no doubt that Lotta Schelin is the best Swedish player ever—and one of the greatest to ever play the game. Period.

Lotta—whose full name is Charlotta Eva—was born in the Swedish capital, Stockholm, in 1984, but her family moved to the outskirts of another major city, Goteburg, when she was a small child. She and her older sister Camilla played soccer from the time they were young girls and grew up in an area that is very enthusiastic about soccer. Goteburg was one of the sites of the 1958 World Cup, made famous because of the emergence of seventeen-year-old Pelé. It is also the home of the Gothia Cup, the largest youth soccer tournament in the world.

Lotta was a good all-around athlete, though she was exceptional at soccer. But as a teenager she developed a spinal problem that sidelined her for a time. She was advised to stop playing soccer, but instead of giving up, she went through intensive strength training of her core and rehabilitation and was able to return to the field.

Tall and slender, Lotta had speed and strength on the field. She debuted for the professional team in Goteburg when she was seventeen and scored eight goals in her first nineteen games! She spent seven years there, earning two scoring titles. She also earned an award for her sportsmanship. She became known as an unselfish player, often looking to pass first before taking a shot herself. She could play wide on the wing or in the middle. She was also a welcoming presence to her teammates; when Hope Solo came to Goteburg to play in 2004, she and Lotta became close friends.

Given the wide pool of talent in Sweden and depth of experience, Lotta didn't make her debut with Sweden's senior national team until 2004, at age twenty, one year after Sweden had made it to the final of the 2003 World Cup, losing to Germany. That performance boosted the popularity of the sport in Sweden.

During the Algarve Cup in Portugal, Lotta was called up to the team as a replacement for a player who had the flu, and she made such an impression with her poise and speed that she stayed with the team. She played in the 2004 Olympics and the disappointing 2007 World Cup, when, for the first time ever, Sweden did not advance out of group play. After that competition, several players retired and a new generation—led by Lotta—gained prominence.

Now the face of her team, Lotta played in the 2008 Olympics in Beijing. Following that tournament, she joined the French professional team Olympique Lyonnais for a transfer fee that was relatively lucrative in the world of women's soccer. Though she battled injuries after the transfer, she eventually helped lead Lyon to back-to-back UEFA titles and showcased her goal-scoring abilities. Her last game for Lyon was a victory in the 2016 Champions League Final. Later in 2016, she returned to Sweden, this time playing for the Swedish champions FC Rosengard.

Lotta helped Sweden finish in third place at the 2011 World Cup in Germany, nabbing two assists and two goals. She and her teammates showed the world that the Swedish squad of the 2010s was a serious contender. That finish qualified her team for a place in the London Olympics the next year, where Sweden lost to France in the quarterfinals.

After that tournament, the Swedish team underwent a big change. Pia Sundhage, who had played for Sweden and coached the United States to two gold medals and a second-place World Cup finish, came home to Sweden to coach the national team.

She made Lotta a co-captain along with Caroline Seger. With Sundhage in charge, the team faced higher expectations. But Lotta wasn't 100 percent healthy, and she played in the 2015 World Cup with persistent knee pain. Without their co-captain at full health, Sweden had disappointing results in the tournament, finishing with three draws before being eliminated in group play in a 4–1 dismantling by Germany.

Sweden and Lotta recovered some pride at the 2016 Olympics in Rio. Though Sweden didn't do much in group play—losing 5–1 to host Brazil—and played an extremely defensive style of soccer, the team advanced to the quarterfinals, where it played the United States. In a stunning upset, Sweden beat the Americans on penalty kicks, marking the first time that the U.S. team had failed to advance to the gold medal game.

After the game, American goalkeeper and Lotta's old friend Hope Solo created a controversy by calling the Swedish team "cowards" for their defensive style of play.

Hope's contract with the U.S. national team was terminated as a result of the controversy. Soon after the game, Hope apologized to her friend for her choice of words. Hope added, in an interview on Swedish TV a few months later, that she felt that Lotta was one of the top attacking players in the world and she had found it odd to see her dropping back into defense.

Over the course of an impressive career, Lotta has deservedly earned that reputation as one of the top attacking players. In fact, some took to calling her "the female Zlatan" after male Swedish soccer star Zlatan Ibrahimovic.

Lotta said the comparisons with one of the best players in the world were nice.

"But although he inspires me and I love watching him play, there are big differences between us, too," Lotta said.

"And I like that young girls look up to me as Lotta Schelin. Not as 'the female Zlatan.'"

STATISTICS:

Position: forward
Olympic silver medalist (2016)
174 appearances for the Swedish national team
86 goals

SISSI

I shouted to tell everybody that we were
there, that our work deserved to be respected,
to make them recognize our abilities.

—Sissi

The Brazilian women's soccer team has been dominated by one player—Marta—for so long, that sometimes it's hard to remember that the team had a history of excellence before she arrived.

Before Marta, there was Sissi. When Marta was born, Sissi was already nineteen years old and had been battling boys on the street and male-dominated society on the field, while trying to prove herself in her nation's favorite sport.

When Sissi, whose full name is Sisleide Lima do Amor, was young, it was illegal for her to play soccer. Brazil actually had a law banning girls and women from playing the game, not just professionally, but also in schools or even for fun. The law stated that the sport was incompatible with the female nature. The ban wasn't lifted until 1979, when Sissi was twelve years old.

But Sissi broke that law! She played the game growing up in Bahia. She destroyed her dolls, using their heads as soccer balls since she didn't own the real thing. Finally, her parents bought her a soccer ball, which not only helped keep her dolls intact but also meant the boys had to let her play with them because she owned the ball.

When Sissi was just fourteen, only two years after the ban on female soccer was lifted, she left her home to play professionally in Salvador, Brazil. Though there were some professional women's teams, they were considered the poor sisters of the men's teams, with little backing or funding, often folding after a season and leaving their players unemployed. Sissi joined the Brazilian national team in 1988, two years after it was formed. Brazil finished third in what was then called the FIFA Women's Invitation Tournament or the International Women's Football Tournament.

Sissi also played professionally for clubs in São Paulo through the 1990s. She was not able to participate in the 1991 World Cup, because her team would not release her.

In those early years, the Brazilian national team struggled, lacking support from its nation and federation. The individual members of the team only got together for tournaments, and the lack of chemistry and cohesion was apparent. At the 1991 and 1995 World Cups the team finished ninth. But by the 1996 Olympics, Brazil had jumped up to a fourth-place finish. It gained notice and began receiving better funding from the soccer federation and sponsorship money from Nike.

Sissi was already thirty-two when she earned fame in the 1999 Women's World Cup in Pasadena, California. Easy to spot on the field because of her close-cropped hair and No. 10 jersey—an honor for any Brazilian to wear the number made famous by Pelé—Sissi led Brazil in that World Cup to the semifinals. The left-footed talent was the leading scorer of the tournament with seven goals and shared the Golden Boot award with China's Sun Wen.

Her scoring total was somewhat surprising because Sissi was used to being the one who created opportunities for others to score rather than being on the receiving end.

"I was never a player who scored a lot of goals," Sissi said. "My role was more about setting them up. Even I was surprised when I started scoring freely at that World Cup. I was the playmaker, not the one who finished moves off."

In the 105th minute of the quarterfinals, Sissi scored on a curving free kick against Nigeria. The golden goal won the game and put Brazil in the semifinals against the United States.

"Recalling it still gives me goose bumps," Sissi said. "It was the experience of a lifetime."

After scoring that goal against Nigeria, Sissi ran wildly around the field and pulled her jersey over her head—a move that would famously be reenacted later in the tournament by American Brandi Chastain.

"At that moment, I shouted to tell everybody that we were there," she said. "That our work deserved to be respected. To make them recognize our abilities."

Her national team coach Wilson Oliveira Rica said, "For Brazil, she is the best in the world. For us, Sissi is the queen of soccer."

As if her accomplishments weren't astounding enough, Sissi was playing the tournament at a disadvantage—she was injured.

"Before the World Cup I suffered a facial trauma," she said. "They considered the option of surgery, but I was against it because I didn't want to miss the World Cup. I played with broken bones in my face and luckily I didn't have any problems."

Undeterred by her injury, Sissi continued to compete. But in the semifinals, the Brazilians lost 2–0 to the United States and Sissi was marked tightly by Michelle Akers in the game at Stanford. Though she lost the game, she had found a new home. Sissi soon became a permanent resident of the San Francisco Bay Area.

When the WUSA was formed in 2001, Sissi joined the San Jose CyberRays and helped them win the league title in their inaugural year. She stayed with them until the league shut down. She kept playing in California, spending four years, including one alongside World Cup star Brandi Chastain, on the Storm of the WPSL. When the WPS was launched, she acted as assistant coach for the FC Gold Pride, and—at age forty-two—played in three games.

She continued her coaching career at California high schools and soccer clubs and at a community college. She and her partner helped raise foster children.

Once, Sissi expressed a desire to become the head coach of the Brazilian team.

Sissi's last year with her national team was in 1999. Brazil won the third-place game, beating Norway in the Rose Bowl as the appetizer to the historic final. Brazil had surpassed their expectations for the tournament and had set the stage for the next generation and Marta.

In Brazil and among soccer fans abroad, her legacy lives on. She will forever be remembered as one of the founding figures of professional women's soccer in Brazil.

STATISTICS:

Position: attacking midfielder
World Cup third place (1999)
19 appearances at FIFA tournaments
8 goals at FIFA tournaments

LOUISA NÉCIB

*I love beautiful [soccer]. It's a vehicle for
enjoyment on the pitch. And without
enjoyment, it's impossible to play well.*

—Louisa Nécib

For many years, women's soccer thrived only in certain areas of Europe such as Germany and Scandinavia, which were countries that made strides to be egalitarian cultures in many areas of society.

But women's soccer had a harder time making inroads in the rest of Europe, which tended to view soccer as strictly a male game and belittled women who tried to play the sport.

That started to change in the early twenty-first century, and the change began with France. Leading the French "golden generation" of women, which made a difference in how the sport was viewed, was Louisa Nécib.

Louisa, an attacking midfielder, played a beautiful game. She had excellent vision, possession, passing skills, and touch. As with so many female players who capture the attention of the media, she was immediately labeled "the female Zidane," a comparison to her country's most famous male player. Her nickname was Ziza, a female variant of Zidane's nickname, Zizou.

Like Zidane, Louisa was born in Marseilles to parents of Algerian origin. She grew up playing with boys in her neighborhood and in youth leagues. She played for competitive soccer clubs in Marseilles and on France's national youth teams.

Born in 1987, she was the beneficiary of an initiative in the early 1990s to include girls at the Centre National de Formation et d'Entrainement (the National Center for Education and Training), a high-level training center in Clairefontaine, not far from Paris, which used to be reserved solely for boys. At the center, she took academic classes and played soccer.

Though she was homesick being so far away from her family and almost gave up, Louisa thrived at soccer at the center. She also met girls who would go on to become her future teammates both on the French national team and on her club team in Lyon.

After two years at Clairefontaine, she left to play for Montpellier at age nineteen. During her one season there, she scored eleven goals and helped her team go to the finals of the Challenge de France, where they defeated the Lyon club to win the domestic cup title. Following the season, she signed with the team she'd helped defeat—Lyon. At the time, Lyon was signing up as much young talent as it could in its ultimately successful bid to become the strongest women's team on the European continent.

Olympique Lyonnais is one of the major drivers of women's football in Europe. The women's division of one of the most popular and storied soccer teams in France has been very successful. Beginning in 2004, when it was elevated to Division 1 status, Olympique has won the UEFA women's cup three times.

Its players have made up the core of the French national team. In addition to Louisa, others of the "golden generation" like Camille Abily, Eugénie Le Sommer, Élodie Thomis, and Sarah Bouhaddi all played for Lyon. During her career in Lyon, Louisa helped win nine Division 1 championships.

Yet prior to Louisa's arrival, France's impact on the international scene had not been as profound. Les

Bleues—the nickname of the French national team—had previously only participated in one Women's World Cup, in 2003. But thanks to Louisa and her teammates, they became a force in women's soccer. They qualified for the 2011 World Cup in Germany, scoring fifty goals and conceding none in ten matches.

In Germany, Louisa and her teammates caught the imagination of their country, which had been embarrassed by the men's team at the 2010 World Cup when some of the players had openly revolted against their coach, boycotting training sessions and failing to make it out of group play. The women were a refreshing change, as they made an unexpected run to the semifinals, where they lost to the United States. Louisa was praised for her talent, though she had to leave the third-place match because of an injury.

The French team also finished fourth in the London Olympics in 2012 and appeared poised to challenge the hierarchy of women's soccer. But France—which had moved up in the world rankings to third—had a bumpy road to the quarterfinals, which included losing in a shocking upset to Colombia in a group play match and just barely making it out of the field. In the quarterfinals against Germany, Louisa rose to the occasion and gave her team the lead on a goal in the 64th minute. But Germany tied the match in the 83rd minute and eventually won on penalty kicks. Louisa and her teammates went home early, defeated and having fallen short of expectations.

Louisa married Algerian soccer player Liassine Cadamuro in June 2016, two months before her team would compete at the Rio Olympics. She announced that she would retire from soccer after the games, unwilling to try to balance soccer and a long-distance marriage.

"I made the decision when I realized that I couldn't juggle my private life and my sporting career anymore," she said. "Many people make long-distance relationships work perfectly well for them, but that's not the way I view life."

Louisa's team lost 1–0 to Canada in the quarterfinals in the 2016 Olympics in Brazil, meaning she never got the chance to play in either a World Cup championship or a gold medal match. She retired fairly young at age twenty-nine, still considered the class of her game.

"You can see her departure is going to leave quite a void," said her teammate Camille Abily.

Louisa's retirement announcement means—unless

she has a change of heart—that she won't be competing for France when it hosts the Women's World Cup in 2019.

That's a shame, because the interest in the event and its promise of success in France is largely thanks to the talent and performance of Louisa and the rest of her golden generation.

STATISTICS:

Position: midfielder
145 appearances for the French national team
36 goals

HEGE RIISE

*As a teenager people told me I was very good,
but at first I did not have the courage to say to
myself: "I can be a national team player."*

—Hege Riise

For a while, Norway was the American soccer team's biggest rival. And you can probably thank Hege Riise for that.

It wasn't just that the talented midfielder was such a threat on the soccer field, though she was. It was that Hege came up with a famous victory celebration that infuriated the U.S. women's team and made them want to win even more than they already had.

In the 1995 World Cup in Sweden, Norway was one of the top teams in the tournament, having won the 1993 European Championship. Meanwhile, the Americans were the reigning World Cup champions.

In a semifinal match, the United States lost to

Norway, 1–0. The loss hurt, but so did the Norwegians' postmatch celebration. The players linked hands to ankles and crawled around the field in a human train. Hege had seen a men's team do a similar celebration on television and had suggested it.

"I thought it would be fun," she said.

Needless to say, the American players weren't too happy with the celebration.

That wasn't the end of the Norwegians fun in the 1995 World Cup. In the final against Germany, Hege dribbled past two defenders, lined up, and shot between two others into the far corner of the net. Her goal gave Norway a lead from which Germany would never recover. The solo effort is considered one of the best goals in World Cup history. Hege ended up winning the Golden Ball trophy as the MVP of the tournament.

While much of the world was still trying to figure out what to think of women's soccer back in the 1990s, Norway—a world leader in gender equality on many levels—was already ahead of the curve. Hege and her teammates were national heroes after the World Cup victory. The team was escorted home by Norwegian fighter jets and was greeted by a huge turnout of fans for a celebration at the airport. One in every four Norwegians watched the championship match that year.

Hege was born in 1969 in a town outside Oslo and, like so many players of her generation, played with boys until she was a teenager. She made her debut with the national team when she was twenty and played in the first three Women's World Cups. There's no question she was a pioneer—how many people can say they were *there* the moment a historic new tradition was born?

She was famous for having brilliant vision, for seeing things on the field that no one else did and finding small spaces to tuck the ball through. She was once described as having "six pairs of eyes."

"I was good at reading the game and I was always looking for the final pass going forward," Hege said. "I had an attacking mind-set and I don't think I ever passed the ball backwards much."

She played in the first Women's World Cup game in 1991 against host China. Even though Norway lost badly, Hege remembered the moment as magical, playing in a stadium in front of 65,000 fans.

"I'll remember that game for the rest of my life," she said. "Not for the football or the result, but for the spectators . . . It was then I knew the Women's World Cup could be something really special.

"We always felt that having a World Cup would be a big step for women's football [and] that's the way it proved to be."

Four years later came that special day—and special celebration—as Norway won the World Cup championship in 1995.

"I enjoyed every minute of being out there—I felt like nothing could stop me," Hege said. "Most of the team felt that way. We were in the best shape of our lives and feeling unstoppable."

Hege's team and the United States continued their rivalry over the next few years. The teams met in the semifinal of the 1996 Atlanta Olympics, and the U.S. team beat Norway 2–1 in overtime. There was never a rematch in the 1999 World Cup, because Norway lost to China in the semifinal.

But in the 2000 Olympics in Australia, Norway once again beat the Americans, this time in the gold medal match. At age thirty-one, Hege was instrumental in the overtime victory. She had assists on the first goal, just before the half, and the winning goal, twelve minutes into sudden death.

With the victory, Hege completed a rare hat trick: winning an Olympic gold medal, a World Cup, and a European Championship. She is just one of three women ever to accomplish the feat.

During Hege's time on her team, Norway went 16–16–2 against the United States. Hege also played professionally in Japan for Nikko, where she won two titles, and bounced around to several different teams in Norway. Toward the end of her career, she played with the WUSA's Carolina Courage in the United States. She was a two-time MVP with the Courage and led the team to the WUSA championship in 2002, before tearing her ACL early in the 2003 season.

"She was toward the end of her professional career as a player when the WUSA began, but was one of the smartest, craftiest players and so difficult to mark in the midfield," said Angela Hucles, who played against Hege. "She knew how to make a great defensive play, distribute the ball and find herself in a position to score a goal or create one all in the same play."

Hege retired in 2004 at age thirty-seven and became an athletic trainer for a women's team in

Norway. A year earlier, the Norwegian Football Association named Riise the best female soccer play in Norway's history.

In an ironic turn of events, in 2009, she was hired to be an assistant coach for her old nemesis, the U.S. team, working for head coach Pia Sundhage. She had a role in helping develop the skills of several players, including dynamic American midfielder Carli Lloyd.

Now Hege works with a Norwegian club team as well as a youth national team, where she can teach them about Norway's long tradition of winning. And celebrating in style.

STATISTICS:

Position: midfielder

World Cup champion (1995), runner-up (1991)

Olympic gold medalist (2000), bronze medalist (1996)

188 appearances for the Norwegian national team

58 goals

TOP TEN BEST GOALS IN WOMEN'S SOCCER HISTORY

10. DZSENIFER MAROZSÁN, GERMANY, OLYMPIC GOLD MEDAL GAME, 2016

Germany, a former two-time World Cup winner, proved it was still one of the world's elite teams with a gold medal victory over Sweden in Rio de Janeiro. After a scoreless first half, Dzsenifer, just twenty-four, started the second half with a bang. She found the ball at the top of the box and threaded a hard shot between two defenders and past the reach of the outstretched Swedish goalkeeper to give Germany a 1–0 lead. Germany would win its first gold medal with a 2–1 victory.

9. CHRISTINE SINCLAIR, CANADA, OLYMPIC SEMIFINAL, 2012

In a game considered one of the most exciting ever played, where the lead ping-ponged back and forth, Canada's Sinclair scored three goals—a hat trick. Her third goal, which at the time seemed to secure the upset win for Canada, came on a corner kick. Christine received the cross high in the air with her head and buried the ball into the side netting, out of the reach of goalkeeper Hope Solo. Canada lost that game but won the bronze medal.

8. JOY FAWCETT, USA, WOMEN'S WORLD CUP QUARTERFINAL, 1999

If Joy hadn't scored a goal in the quarterfinal against Germany, the history of women's soccer might have been *very* different. The tournament would have gone on but without the interest that captivated America, produced record ratings, and caught the attention of fans and sponsors around the world. With the score against Germany tied 2–2, Shannon MacMillan subbed in for Julie Foudy. Shannon sent a perfect cross on a corner kick right to the head of Joy, who sent it into the goal. The Americans held on for the win and moved one step closer to making history.

7. **MIA HAMM**, USA, WOMEN'S WORLD CUP GROUP PLAY, 1999

Mia scored so many goals during her legendary career that it's difficult to choose just one to call "her best." But we'll pick her first goal for the American team in the 1999 World Cup, because it started the team's historic, culture-shifting run. Against Denmark, in front of a sold-out crowd at Giants Stadium in New Jersey, where half the fans seemed to be wearing Hamm jerseys, Mia didn't disappoint. In the 17th minute, she received a cross from Brandi Chastain on the right side of the box, popped the ball past one defender, then sent it in with a left-footed blast past the diving Danish goalkeeper, to the delight of the fans.

6. **MICHELLE AKERS**, USA, WOMEN'S WORLD CUP FINAL, 1991

With just minutes to play in the first Women's World Cup final, with the score tied 1–1, Michelle attempted to run down a long pass from a teammate, but the pass was intercepted by a Norwegian defender. With Michelle barreling down on her, the defender attempted a backpass to her goalkeeper. But the pass never got there— Michelle leapt on it, passed it to herself with her left foot, and knocked it into the net with her right foot, scoring her second goal of the match. It proved to be the game-winner as the game ended shortly after, and the United States won its first world championship.

5. CARLI LLOYD, USA, WOMEN'S WORLD CUP FINAL, 2015

Carli's 2015 performance is considered the greatest—male or female—in a World Cup final. She scored a hat trick . . . in just the first sixteen minutes of the match! She effectively won the game for her team in less than one-sixth of regulation time. We have to pick one, so we'll pick her third goal. In the 15th minute, she intercepted the ball at midfield, pushed it ahead of her, and took a full swing—sending a 54-yard rocket toward the net. The ball bounced once, kissed the left post, and rolled into the net. It was a shot Carli had practiced many times, and she perfected it in the biggest moment of her career.

4. **ABBY WAMBACH**, USA, WOMEN'S WORLD CUP QUARTERFINAL, 2011

This is not the most important goal ever scored, and it wasn't even a game-winner, but it's surely the most dramatic goal ever scored. The U.S. women were fighting for their life against Brazil in the 122nd minute, trailing by a goal in a game that had been full of strange events. Desperate to push the ball forward, centerback Christie Rampone passed to defender Ali Krieger, who passed to Carli Lloyd. Instead of dribbling the ball up the field, Carli passed wide to a sprinting Megan Rapinoe. Megan struck the ball with her left foot, sending an arcing cross to the far post, where Abby rose up and slammed the goal in with her head. The goal was the latest ever scored in a World Cup game, men's or women's, and sent the game to penalty kicks, which the U.S. team won.

3.   HOMARE SAWA, JAPAN, WOMEN'S WORLD CUP FINAL, 2011

Homare's goal was a magician's trick—even in super slow motion, it is difficult to see how she scored the overtime goal that tied the score with the United States at 2–2 late in the final. On a Japan corner kick, Homare charged into the box chased by an American defender. She leapt and flicked the ball into the box with her right foot—and it deflected off another American on its way in. The goal set up Japan's stunning penalty kick victory to win the world championship.

2.   MARTA, BRAZIL, WOMEN'S WORLD CUP SEMIFINAL, 2007

In a rout of the favored Americans, Marta trapped the ball high in the box, flicked it past the closest defender, dribbled around another defender, and shot it into the corner. It was the second of four Brazilian goals, so it's not the most important goal ever scored. But it was probably the most breathtaking goal and it announced the arrival of the best player on earth.

1. BRANDI CHASTAIN, USA, WOMEN'S WORLD CUP FINAL, 1999

Technically a penalty kick is not a goal, so we're cheating by including it. But this was arguably the most important score in women's soccer history. With more than 90,000 fans—including the president of the United States—packed into the Rose Bowl and eighteen million more watching at home, the pressure and the stakes were enormous. Chastain balled up the toes on her left foot and rocketed the ball inside the right post. With that kick, the Americans won the World Cup and changed the narrative of women's sports forever.

▶ ▶ ▶ **EXTRA TIME**

THE TOP EVENTS IN THE HISTORY OF WOMEN'S SOCCER

Women's soccer has grown tremendously in the twenty-first century. While there are tournaments all around the world, the biggest events remain the World Cup and the Olympics. We already talked about the first organized international tournaments earlier on. Now here's a look at the most famous events in the history of women's soccer.

I. THE 1999 WORLD CUP IN THE UNITED STATES

Some sports have grown gradually over time, in fits and starts. Others explode in popularity after a monumental occasion takes place. The story of the growth of women's soccer is one of explosion.

The 1999 World Cup was undoubtedly the turning point for women's soccer, the moment when it became a heavyweight player in the sports world.

The American organizers had to convince FIFA

that the event could be held in huge stadiums, the same places where America's most popular sport, football, took place.

The head of the organizing committee, a woman named Marla Messing, was sure that the event would sell lots of tickets. She saw the huge untapped market of youth soccer. She had the support of the players on the American team, who were always trying to grow their sport. The unexpectedly large crowds from the 1996 Olympics gave them faith that the World Cup would be a huge success.

"You had to sell it as a major event," Messing said.

Ignored by major sponsors and even FIFA itself, Messing oversaw an untraditional marketing effort, going directly to youth soccer tournaments to recruit fans and sending direct-mail information to coaches, leagues, and parents. Six months before the event, her organization had already sold 200,000 tickets.

Still, no one was fully prepared for the scene at the opener in June against Denmark at the Meadowlands, the New York Giants and Jets stadium in East Rutherford, New Jersey. Traffic was snarled for miles. The parking lot was packed hours before the game started. And the crowd of 78,972 was wildly enthusiastic.

From that game on, the World Cup gained momentum. The American players became famous, appearing on late-night television, in TV commercials, and in the most popular magazines nationwide. The media was fully on board, and suddenly Women's World Cup matches had a spotlight shined on them like never before. The crowds continued to be huge: more than 65,000 in Chicago; more than 54,000 in Washington, D.C.; more than 73,000 for a semifinal at Stanford. The team was like a bandwagon, gathering fans and followers as it rolled on through the summer of 1999.

The championship game against China, on a sweltering July day at the Rose Bowl, drew the kind of numbers that no one would have believed possible a few months earlier. A crowd of 90,185 packed the building. Included in the crowd was President Bill Clinton. The television ratings were phenomenal: 17.98 million viewers tuned in to the game.

"All I could see was a sea of people," Kristine Lilly said. "I could have bawled. We had been waiting so long for people to come and watch us."

Then came victory for the Americans and one of the most iconic moments in the history of sports:

Brandi Chastain's unforgettable celebration after her successful penalty kick.

In the aftermath of the game, celebrations spread across America like wildfire. Thousands of words were written about the meaning of the event. There was a very real sense that the world of sports had somehow shifted. There had been great American female athletes before, but for the first time, there was a historic American women's sports team that mesmerized and mobilized the nation.

II. THE 2000 SYDNEY OLYMPICS

One year after the 1999 World Cup, the women's soccer world hoped to continue the momentum at the Sydney Olympics in Australia. For the first time, there was a real eagerness among the American and international media to cover women's soccer. The American players were considered some of the biggest stars at the Olympics.

While the attendance for the games didn't match the American crowds from previous Olympics in Atlanta or the 1999 World Cup—perhaps because the games were played outside Sydney and the Australian team was an underdog—the crowds were strong and enthusiastic. The American team cruised through group play, fueled by familiar names like Mia Hamm, Brandi Chastain, and Julie Foudy. The U.S. team beat Brazil 1–0 in the semifinal, setting up a final against Norway, the team that had beaten the Americans in the final of the 1995 World Cup.

Norway came into the game with a winning record against the mighty U.S. team, despite having lost 2–0 to the Americans in group play. More important, they had the drive and a gritty sense of determination. The Americans scored right away, but the Norwegians tied the score just before the half and took the lead midway through the second half. At the end of regulation play, American forward Tiffeny Milbrett headed in her second goal of the match to tie the score.

Overtime!

Rules at the time dictated that a "golden goal" would decide the match, meaning that the first goal in overtime would win the game. But no one knew that goal would come on such a bizarre play—and that a bit of controversy would follow.

Twelve minutes into overtime, in a sequence of events that resembled a game of hot potato, a pass from

Norwegian star Hege Riise hit off American defender Joy Fawcett's head and ricocheted onto Norwegian Dagny Mellgren's upper arm and onto the ground, where Mellgren met it and shot it into the goal.

Though the goal was disputed as a hand ball, it stood, while the Americans fell.

"I don't want to focus on that," Julie Foudy said of the play after the match. "I think we need to applaud Norway for a great game."

Norway had won gold. The U.S. had won silver. And though a rivalry for the ages seemed to be forming, that was actually the last time the teams met in a championship final.

III. THE 2003 WORLD CUP IN THE UNITED STATES

Everything about the 2003 World Cup was strange. And it's that strangeness, even more so than the thrilling matches that unfolded, that made this World Cup a memorable event in history.

The tournament was supposed to be held in China but there were global concerns because of the SARS outbreak in that country. SARS was a serious respiratory syndrome that infected eight thousand people in China and caused over seven hundred deaths. The decision to move the tournament was made just four months before the scheduled start and the logical choice was for the United States to be the emergency host, since the country had hosted the 1999 World Cup.

The American hosts were scrambling at the last minute to find venues and put together a schedule. There were concerns from the start that because of the emergency organization, there was no chance that the tournament would be as big a success as 1999, and would therefore be perceived as a step backward for women's soccer.

Still, the struggling professional soccer league— the WUSA—hoped that the World Cup would give their league a boost and showcase its players.

Instead, the opposite happened. Just five days before the tournament was set to begin on September 20, the WUSA announced it was ceasing operations. The news was a huge blow to all the teams participating, but in particular to the American team, whose players were the founding members of the league. They had invested their hearts and souls into trying to build it. They were understandably upset, yet had to rally to try to win a World Cup.

The U.S. team cruised through the group play, winning all three of their games, and beat rival Norway 1–0 in the quarterfinals. But in the semifinal, the Americans were crushed by Germany, 3–0. Germany went on to win its first World Cup title, beating Sweden 2–1 in the final.

All in all, it was a disappointing finish for the Americans. But despite the bizarre circumstances, the 2003 World Cup kept the momentum going in America for women's soccer, further building off the foundation established by the 1999 squad. Clearly, a bright future was ahead.

IV. THE 2004 ATHENS OLYMPICS

Athens was the last hurrah for some of the greatest players to ever play the game. Mia Hamm, Julie Foudy, and Joy Fawcett—three women who helped put women's soccer on the map—announced before the tournament that they would be retiring following the competition. That news sparked a great sense of urgency, as the U.S. hadn't won a championship since the 1999 World Cup. No one knew what the next generation would bring, though Abby Wambach had begun to establish herself as a rising star.

The time to win, many thought, was *now*.

The U.S. team got through group play with two wins and a surprising draw against Australia. It beat Japan in the quarterfinals and then faced powerful Germany in the semifinal on the Greek island of Crete. The Americans went up early but allowed an equalizing goal in extra time. In overtime, midfielder Heather O'Reilly scored to put the U.S. team back in the gold medal game, against Brazil.

The Athens Olympics was the debut of Brazil's Marta in the international spotlight. And though Brazil was a much-improved team and outplayed the American team for most of the game, the gold medal seemed destined for Hamm and company. It was neck-and-neck from start to finish, and the two teams needed extra time to decide the match. Finally, in the 112th minute, Abby Wambach won the game with a header, a signal of the changing of the guard.

"It's a fabulous way to win an Olympic gold medal," Wambach said. "And it's an even better way to send off these women, because they're what this is about."

After the game, the five players left from the 1991 World Cup—Mia Hamm, Julie Foudy, Joy Fawcett, Brandi Chastain, and Kristine Lilly—wrapped their arms around one another on the medal podium as they received their medals and listened to the anthem. It was the end of an era.

V. THE 2007 WORLD CUP IN CHINA

With apologies to eventual champion Germany—which became the first team to win consecutive Women's World Cups—the 2007 World Cup in China is often primarily remembered for two things other than the winner: Hope Solo and Marta.

The 2007 World Cup was held in China, the country that had to give up hosting the 2003 World Cup because of an outbreak of SARS that had spread throughout the country. The Americans came in as the top-ranked team and had not lost a game in forty-seven outings prior to the World Cup. Still, most of the '99ers—as the winning World Cup team was known—were gone, replaced by a group of young, talented, and significantly less famous players. This caused Nike to start an ad campaign with the theme "The Greatest Team You've Never Heard Of."

The new team entered the tournament determined to make a name for itself.

The U.S. team had a draw against North Korea in its first game, when Abby Wambach left the field to get stitches in her head and North Korea scored two quick goals while the Americans played a player short. The U.S. team came back in the match and salvaged the tie, then won the next two games of group play and the quarterfinal against England.

Hope Solo had been in goal for almost all of the Americans' extraordinary unbeaten streak and had been the starting goalkeeper for more than two years. But coach Greg Ryan decided to bench her for the semifinal against Brazil and put in former starter Briana Scurry, who hadn't been the No. 1 goalkeeper in three years. The result was a disaster, with the U.S. losing 4–0.

Brazil's new star Marta was a dazzling presence on the field, a constant threat, scoring two goals.

Afterward, Solo told the press about her benching, "It was the wrong decision, and I think anybody that knows anything about the game knows that."

Back home in the United States, it became a huge controversy: a female athlete criticizing her coach was almost unheard-of. In China, Solo's remarks were interpreted as criticizing Scurry, and her teammates ostracized her, not letting her eat with them or even fly home with them. It was a huge and very public divide on a very popular team.

Despite Marta's fabulous performance throughout the World Cup, Germany put on an impressive display, right from their first match, when they destroyed Argentina 11–0. It was the largest margin of defeat and the most goals ever scored in a single Women's World Cup match. From there, they progressed to the finals, where they ultimately beat Marta and Brazil. Germany won with the combined stellar play of goalkeeper Nadine Angerer, who didn't give up a goal in the tournament, and Birgit Prinz, who scored five goals.

Meanwhile, the frustrated American squad left China with a rift to repair and much work to be done if they wanted a chance to redeem themselves at the Olympics in Beijing.

VI. THE 2008 BEIJING OLYMPICS

Eleven months after the 2007 World Cup, the women's soccer world was back in China for the Beijing Olympics. And the Americans were trying to regroup.

They had a new coach, former Swedish star

player Pia Sundhage, who replaced fired coach Greg Ryan after the World Cup disaster. She brought the U.S. team—including Hope Solo—together and told the players it was a new era and that Hope was the goalkeeper.

But then disaster struck.

On the final game of the team's farewell tour before leaving for the Olympics, against Brazil in San Diego, Abby Wambach shattered her leg. The team's biggest star would miss the Olympics.

The American team started poorly, losing 2–0 to Norway. But after that game ended, they put the loss out of their minds, shook off the rust, and never looked back—and they didn't lose another game in the tournament.

Even without their leader, the team beat Japan and New Zealand and advanced to the quarterfinals, where it defeated Canada 2–1 in overtime. In the semifinal, the Americans beat Japan once more to make it to the gold medal match, where they faced off against Brazil—the team that had knocked the United States out of the World Cup in China.

In the championship match, Solo made some amazing saves, including a point-blank one on a shot at goal by Marta, blocked with her arm. The game went to extra time and Carli Lloyd scored a goal early. Marta had several more chances, but Solo stopped them all and the United States won 1–0.

Afterward Solo said, "It's unreal to me. It's like a storybook ending."

Hope Solo, and America, had reclaimed glory.

VII. THE 2011 WORLD CUP IN GERMANY

When Germany hosted the World Cup, it had a different feel. A hard-core soccer country that had hosted the men's World Cup just five years earlier was hosting the women's biggest event, and everything about the tournament was organized and first-class.

The host country was the two-time reigning World Cup champion and was expected to battle with the favored United States for a chance to win three in a row. What no one could predict was the power of emotion that swept Japan into the final.

As expected, both Germany and the United States made it through group play, with Germany undefeated and the Americans losing one game to Sweden. The quarterfinal match between the U.S. team and Brazil was epic and will long be remembered as one of the great matches in World Cup history.

The United States went up 1–0, but in the second half, American Rachel Buehler tackled Marta in the penalty box. Buehler was sent off, leaving the Americans shorthanded, and Brazil was awarded a penalty kick. Hope Solo saved it, but the referee called encroachment on one of the U.S. players and ordered a rekick, which was successful. Regulation play ended in a tie, but then Brazil went ahead early in overtime. In the 122nd minute, with time running out for the United States, Megan Rapinoe brought the ball down the field and sent a laserlike 30-foot crossing pass to the net. Abby Wambach launched herself at the ball and headed it into the goal as time expired!

In penalty kicks, as it almost always does, it came down to the goalkeepers. Solo saved one while Brazilian goalkeeper Andreia saved none.

The U.S. team advanced and was a game away from the finals.

Germany wasn't so lucky. The two-time champions were knocked out by Japan, 1–0, in a shocker.

Both Japan and the United States won their semifinal matches by the score of 3–1, Japan over Sweden and the United States over rising power France. That set up a final few could have predicted. But then, no one could foresee the emotion of the Japanese team, whose country had suffered a devastating earthquake and tsunami four months earlier. Close to twenty thousand people were dead, and hundreds of thousands more displaced from their homes.

At every game, the Japanese team unfurled a sign that read, *To our friends around the world – thank you for your support*, and the players bowed in respect. They felt it was their mission to bring joy to their nation, and back home they were embraced not only for their success but for their aesthetically pleasing, quick-passing style of play.

Against the United States, Japan was resilient. Though the U.S. team dominated play and went up early, Japan didn't quit and came back to tie it. In overtime, the Americans took the lead again, but once more the Japanese team came back, led by its fearless leader Homare Sawa, and fueled by the support and suffering of their nation.

The game went to penalty kicks, but the Americans missed one kick and had two others saved. Japan, the huge underdog, won an emotional victory.

The final game received huge television ratings around the world and set a then-record on Twitter for tweets per second, at 7,196.

Back in Tokyo, fans poured out into the street to celebrate. It had been too long since they'd had a reason to smile.

VIII. THE 2012 LONDON OLYMPICS

The London Olympics was a chance for women's soccer to take the stage in another serious soccer country. While England prides itself on being the birthplace of the game, the women's game has struggled for recognition there. At the beginning of the London Olympics, some British media members were openly scoffing at the prospect that anyone would attend the women's games held at some of soccer's most iconic stadiums.

They changed their tune early on, when the crowds were strong, and more than 70,000 fans packed historic Wembley Stadium to see Great Britain defeat Brazil 1–0.

The American team was hitting on all cylinders and cruised through group play, as did the surprising team from Great Britain. But then Great Britain's exciting run was cut short by Canada, setting up a memorable semifinal at Old Trafford in Manchester against the United States.

In what some called "the greatest game of women's soccer ever played"—which might be hyperbole—Canada's Christine Sinclair scored a hat trick. But after each one of Sinclair's three goals, the Americans came back to tie the game, including on a controversial penalty kick, awarded due to a disputed hand ball against Canada. The hand ball came on a free kick, awarded because of another controversial call for delay of game. In other words, the game was very contentious. In the 123rd minute, Alex Morgan headed home the game-winner, though the Canadian players bitterly complained about the outcome.

The gold medal game was a rematch between Japan and the United States. The Americans got redemption, thanks to two goals by Carli Lloyd and several saves by Hope Solo, in the 2-1 victory. The game was played at Wembley before 80,203 people, a new Olympic record for attendance.

With another win under their belt, the latest generation of American stars began to draw comparisons to the epic team that had won the World Cup in 1999.

IX. THE 2015 WORLD CUP IN CANADA

The Canadian World Cup was the largest ever, with twenty-four teams involved, up from sixteen in the previous competition. It also began with controversy, because of the fact that all the venues were surfaced with artificial grass, which many players thought would increase their chances of getting injured. Several players, led by Abby Wambach, brought a lawsuit against FIFA, soccer's governing body, charging gender discrimination because their male counterparts played on real grass. The players eventually dropped the claim, understanding that it wouldn't be resolved before the World Cup and concerned that it would be a distraction from their efforts.

In group play, only Brazil and Japan got through unscathed. Host Canada struggled, as did the United States, which had a hard time finding its stride under new coach Jill Ellis. In group play, the U.S. team had an emotional matchup against Sweden, led by their former coach Pia Sundhage, who had resigned to coach her home team following the London Olympics. Going into the match, there were some hard feelings from the

Americans after Pia gave an interview to the *New York Times* days earlier in which she criticized some of her former players. The match, just like the war of words that followed the interview, ended in a tie.

The U.S. team beat Colombia and China in the first two knockout rounds, setting up a match between two heavyweights in the semifinal, with number-one-ranked Germany. The Americans played with newfound aggressiveness, though the outcome of the game came down to penalty kicks awarded during the game. The Germans missed one and Carli Lloyd made one against noted penalty kick stopper Nadine Angerer. Kelley O'Hara scored the deciding goal that put the United States back into the World Cup final.

For the third straight major championship, the Americans met Japan, which had officially established itself as a force in women's soccer, in the final. But this game was not to be a tense battle like the previous two. The game was held in Vancouver, a short drive from the U.S. border, and the crowd was wildly pro-U.S.A. Carli Lloyd channeled all that energy into an astonishing performance, scoring a goal just three minutes into the game and adding two more in the first sixteen minutes. Lauren Holiday, who had joined the team in 2008 after replacing an injured Abby Wambach, added another, and the Americans had a 4–0 lead before the first half was even halfway over. Japan fought back to cut the deficit to 4–2, but when midfielder Tobin Heath added another goal in the second half, the result was secured. It was the last game for striker Abby Wambach—and the perfect way to end her illustrious career.

The 5–2 victory gave the United States its third World Cup Championship and its first since the signature moment in 1999. The final shattered TV ratings for previous soccer games, with 25.4 million viewers tuning in to make it the most-watched soccer game—male or female—in U.S. history.

X. THE 2016 RIO OLYMPICS

There was plenty of heartbreak to go around at the Rio Olympics, but Germany declined a serving. After several disappointing years, the Germans reasserted themselves as one of the top teams by claiming their first ever Olympic gold medal.

Most of the heartbreak belonged to Marta and her Brazilian teammates, who hoped to help grow support in their country with a showcase on their home turf.

Their prospects seemed promising at first as Brazil advanced to the quarterfinals and beat Australia on penalty kicks. That victory put them in a semifinal in iconic Maracanã Stadium in Rio de Janeiro, one of Brazil's most famous cities, where the final would also be played.

Attendance numbers had been underwhelming at most of the early matches, played in cities outside Rio. But in the semifinal, 70,000 people packed Maracanã—the biggest crowd to ever watch women's soccer in Brazil—and many wore Marta's No. 10 jersey. But Sweden's defensive style suffocated the Brazilian offense, and Brazil fell on penalty kicks.

Sweden, which went on to lose to Germany in the final, had played spoiler again. In the quarterfinals, Sundhage's team knocked out the reigning gold medalist Americans, beating her former squad 4–3 on penalty kicks. After the game, Hope Solo created a stir by saying the Swedes played "like cowards." Though she clarified that she meant their style of play, she was eventually suspended by U.S. Soccer for her remarks and had her contract terminated.

The result was the first time the U.S. team had failed to advance to the Olympic gold medal game and signaled that the team would need to rebuild and regroup before the 2019 World Cup in France.

CONCLUSION

In its short yet eventful history, women's soccer has seen the rise and fall of giants, the improbable victories of underdogs, and the growth of young players in every corner of the world. With such an impressive past, one can only wonder at the greatness yet to come. One thing is for certain: there's plenty more women's soccer to be played and world-class talent to be discovered.

UPCOMING EVENTS:

2019 WOMEN'S WORLD CUP

Host: France

Venues in nine cities: Paris, Lyon, Rennes, Le Havre, Valenciennes, Reims, Montpellier, Nice, Grenoble

Dates: June 1–30, 2019

2020 SUMMER OLYMPICS

Host: Tokyo

Dates: July 24 to August 9, 2020

2023 WOMEN'S WORLD CUP

Host: TBD

Dates: TBD

2024 SUMMER OLYMPICS

Host: Paris

Dates: TBD

TOP TEN BIGGEST UPSETS
IN WOMEN'S SOCCER HISTORY

10. **NORWAY 1, USA 0**, 1995 WOMEN'S WORLD CUP

    The Americans were the reigning World Cup champions and one year away from becoming the first Olympic gold medalists. But they were frustrated and stymied by Norway in a semifinal game in Vasteras, Sweden. Norway's Ann Kristin Aarones scored in the 10th minute, and the game became a defensive battle. Norway was one of the few teams that wasn't intimidated by the Americans' firepower and wasn't matched up physically. Aarones's goal was all Norway needed to earn the victory. Norway went on to beat Germany in the final, while the U.S. players used the defeat as motivation to fuel them for the next several years.

9. **NIGERIA 1, SWEDEN 1**, 2007 WOMEN'S WORLD CUP

    In the early days of women's soccer Nigeria was the best team in Africa, winning the first seven African championships. But once the team got outside its continent, it had trouble competing. Its best finish came in the 1999 World Cup, when Nigeria advanced to the quarterfinals. But in 2007, Nigeria sent shock waves through the soccer world with a tie against Sweden, one of the favorites that year. Stuck in a "group of death" with top teams like the United States, Sweden, and North Korea, Nigeria managed a tie with Sweden when Cynthia Uwak scored an equalizing goal with eight minutes left to play. That momentarily threw the group into confusion, as North Korea and the United States had also tied. After their shocking victory, Nigeria fell back to earth and didn't score again throughout the rest of the tournament, finishing last in its group.

8. NORWAY 3, USA 2, 2000 SYDNEY OLYMPICS

Still soaring from their World Cup championship fourteen months earlier, the American team arrived at the Olympics as full-fledged stars. In the team's opening match, the U.S.

team easily dispatched Norway 2–0, prompting many to assume their onetime rivalry was dead. But Norway recovered from that defeat to make it to the semifinals, where it defeated Germany, setting up a rematch with the Americans in the gold medal match. Twice Norway took a lead, and twice American Tiffeny Milbrett tied it up. Twelve minutes into sudden-death overtime, the ball ricocheted off the upper body of Norway's Dagny Mellgren. Mellgren chased the ball down and shot it into the U.S. goal to end the game. It was the perfect revenge following their loss earlier in the tournament. The referee ignored complaints by the Americans about a hand ball on the winning goal.

7. COLOMBIA 2, FRANCE 0, 2015 WOMEN'S WORLD CUP

Coming into the World Cup in Canada, France was a trendy pick to win it all. The French were ranked third and had been semifinalists four years earlier in Germany. But in group play, Colombia crafted a huge upset in New Brunswick. Lady Andrade scored in the 19th minute and goalkeeper Sandra Sepulveda held the French at bay. An extra time goal by Catalina Usme sealed the win. Colombia was helped by officiating controversy when a handball was not called. Despite the victory, France won the group and advanced to the quarterfinals, while Colombia lost to the United States in the round of 16.

6. **MEXICO 2, USA 1**, 2010 WORLD CUP QUALIFYING MATCH

Called "one of the biggest upsets in sports history," Mexico's first win over the United States in November 2010 put the Americans' chances at making the 2011 World Cup in peril. Mexico scored first in the game held in Cancun, Mexico, when Maribel Dominguez found the net in the 3rd minute. Carli Lloyd tied the score twenty-two minutes later. But in the 27th minute, Veronica Perez beat goalkeeper Nicole Barnhart, starting in place of the injured Hope Solo, who had recently had shoulder surgery. The loss was stunning, forcing the U.S. team to wait until weeks later to qualify for the World Cup, doing so in dramatic fashion by beating Italy in a play-in game.

5. **CANADA 1, CHINA 0**, 2003 WOMEN'S WORLD CUP

In the aftermath of the 1999 World Cup, China was clearly a team expected to dominate in the future. Sun Wen was one of the best players in the world. The team had support and backing and high expectations. But in the World Cup that China was supposed to host, the Chinese team was unexpectedly ousted in the quarterfinals by upstart Canada. Veteran Charmaine Hooper scored the only goal in the game in Portland, Oregon, and goalkeeper Taryn Swiatek and the defense in front of her were strong, frustrating China's attack. China went home and Canada went on to the semifinals.

4. **SWEDEN 0, BRAZIL 0 (SWEDEN WINS 4–3 ON PENALTY KICKS)**, 2016 RIO OLYMPICS

The Swedes, with their defensive mind-set, took out a favorite in the Olympic semifinal, just days after ousting the favored Americans.

Brazil and Sweden had already met in group play with Brazil decimating the Swedes 5-1. But Sweden had a different tactic heading into the semifinal. Despite constant pressure by Marta—who had scored a hat trick in the earlier game against Sweden—and her teammates during 120 minutes of regulation play and extra time at a packed Maracanã Stadium in Rio, Brazil could not score against the loaded Swedish defense. In penalty kicks, the teams stayed even until Swedish goalkeeper Hedvig Lindahl saved an attempt by Andressinha. Then Lisa Dahlkvist converted her kick to send Sweden to the gold medal game.

3. **GERMANY 3, USA 0,** 2003 WOMEN'S WORLD CUP

Four years after making women's sports history, the U.S. team was full of recognized names and was a heavy favorite to repeat as champion. But those dreams ended in a semifinal game in Portland, Oregon, when the Americans came out hesitant against Germany's powerful defense and couldn't rally despite increasing desperation. Kerstin

Garefrekes gave Germany a 1–0 lead on a corner kick header, which held up until extra time of the second half, when German stars Maren Meinert and Birgit Prinz scored the 1–2 knockout blows. Germany went on to win the World Cup, while the Americans finished third.

2. JAPAN 1, GERMANY 0, 2011 WOMEN'S WORLD CUP

Germany was the host country of the 2011 World Cup and the two-time defending world champion. Japan, though ranked fourth in the world, was a tiny team given little chance of competing against the world power. But the Japanese players, fueled by the emotion surrounding their country's devastating earthquake and tsunami, controlled the pace of the game played in Wolfsburg, Germany. They connected passes with precision and smothered any German counterattack hopes. In the 108th minute of extra time, Homare Sawa angled a shot past German goalkeeper Nadine Angerer, for the lone goal of the quarterfinal match. Japan would go on to win the World Cup, while Germany was left to regroup.

1. SWEDEN 1, USA 1 (SWEDEN WINS 4–3 ON PENALTY KICKS), 2016 RIO OLYMPICS

The defending World Cup champions had a fully loaded team and a determination to become the first team to be both World Cup champions and Olympic gold medalists in consecutive years. The Americans had made it through group play with two wins and a draw, while Sweden had a 1–1–1 record. The U.S. team dominated the game, outshooting Sweden 27–6. But Sweden took the first lead on a counterattack goal by Stina Blackstenius. Alex Morgan came back to tie it. After two periods of extra time, the game went to penalty kicks. Morgan's kick was saved and Christen Press sent hers over the goal. Hope Solo saved one of Sweden's kicks, but she and her teammates came up short. It was the first time the American team did not medal, and the first time it failed to advance to at least the semifinal of a major tournament.

▶ ▶ ▶ **PENALTY KICKS**

THE NEXT GENERATION OF SUPERSTARS

Women's soccer is evolving—quickly. As we have learned in previous chapters, the sport is relatively young as an organized, competitive enterprise. But growth and progress have come quickly. The talent pool continues to expand and players' skill level keeps getting higher and higher.

We've taken a look at some of the legends of the game. Now it's time to take a look at some of the players projected to be stars in the coming years. Predictions are always difficult, because one can't know what obstacles or injuries a player might face along the way. But the future of women's soccer is very bright.

Here is a look at Generation Next: the players who could be raising trophies and making history in the years ahead. There are plenty we don't yet know about. Maybe even you!

MALLORY PUGH, USA

. . . .

Background: "Mal" is considered the next breakout star for the U.S. women's national team. At just seventeen, the forward made her debut with the senior national team in January 2016 and scored against Ireland. She was included on the roster for the 2016 Rio Olympics and scored a goal against Colombia. The Colorado native had committed to play for UCLA in 2017 but sat out the fall semester in order to participate in the under-20 World Cup. The next spring, Mal decided to pursue a professional career rather than play in college, signing with the Washington Spirit of the NWSL.

Skill set: Speed, vision, elusiveness. Good with her head. Often compared to Mia Hamm as a potential future star of her generation.

Breakout moment: In her first game with the senior team, in January 2016, Mal scored a goal against Ireland. She was the second runner toward the goal, following Christen Press, who crossed the ball to her. Mal put her head on it and knocked it in. She's been a fixture on the senior team since.

SOPHIA SMITH, USA

. . . .

Background: Like Mal, Sophia is another rising star forward out of Colorado. U.S. coach Jill Ellis called Sophia into the senior team training camp when she was just sixteen. When she was just a junior in high school, Sophia scored five goals in three games for the under-18 team. That earned her a spot on the U-20 team, where she scored four goals in three games. The seven-week scoring barrage earned Sophia a chance to play with the senior team camp in 2017. Sophia is headed to play college ball at Stanford.

Skill set: Quickness, skill in tight spaces. A pure forward, Sophia has a nose for the goal.

Breakout moment: On tour with the under-18 team in England, Sophia scored twice against England and followed that up with a hat trick in a win over Norway. Jill Ellis took note and called Sophia into camp a few weeks later.

ROSE LAVELLE, USA

. . . .

Background: A midfielder who grew up in Cincinnati,

Ohio, Rose played college ball at Wisconsin. She played on the American U-18, U-20, and U-23 teams and was called in to train with the senior team in 2015. She made her first appearance with the national team in 2017, against England in the SheBelieves Cup, and was named player of the match. She quickly became a fixture on the national team. Rose was the first pick of the 2017 NWSL draft, by the Boston Breakers.

Skill set: Vision, calm presence, fluidity, left-footed. Great change of direction. Considered the heir apparent to Carli Lloyd.

Breakout moment: In her debut at the SheBelieves Cup, she was named player of the match in the 1–0 loss, exhibiting her ball control and poise.

JANE CAMPBELL, USA

Background: Tapped as the possible goalkeeper of the future, following in the footsteps of Hope Solo and Briana Scurry, Campbell played college ball at Stanford. She set a record at Stanford for goalkeeping minutes played and tied former national team player Nicole Barnhart for career shutouts. The native of Georgia received a national team camp invitation at age seventeen, becoming one of the youngest players to be called into the full team camp. Though she had not made her debut with the national team as of mid-2017, Jane is considered perhaps the most promising young goalkeeper available to Jill Ellis. She plays professionally for the Houston Dash.

Skill set: Physical and confident, she is known for shot-stopping ability. Has been compared to Solo.

Breakout moment: Jane led Stanford for four years. In her senior year, she started off with a bang to make four saves to earn a shutout against No. 6 Florida. A few weeks later, Jill Ellis called her back into the national team camp.

HINA SUGITA, JAPAN

. . . .

Background: An up-and-coming global star, the midfielder, at nineteen years old, earned the Golden Ball at the U-20 World Cup in 2016, as the best player in the tournament. She also had been named the best player of the 2014 U-17 World Cup, leading Japan to the title and acting as team captain. She plays professionally for Kobe Leonessa.

Skill set: Quick and precise on offense, Hina is also

a solid defender. Because of her poise, she has been called the successor to Homare Sawa.

Breakout moment: In a 10–0 rout over Panama at the U-17, Hina scored a hat trick. She led her team to the championship.

MAMI UENO, JAPAN
. . . .

Background: The forward earned the Golden Boot at the U-20 World Cup, scoring the most goals, five. Her goal in the 87th minute of the third-place game knocked out the United States. It was her first major tournament and she was surprised to win the Golden Boot. Her rise, along with teammate Hina Sugita, holds promise for the future of the Japanese team.

Skill set: Strong shot, good vision, hard worker.

Breakout moment: At her first major tournament, in the U-20 World Cup in 2016, Mami was a breakout star, scoring a hat trick against Nigeria.

MARIA CALDENTEY, SPAIN
. . . .

Background: The forward, born in 1996 and raised in the Balearic Islands in the Mediterranean, plays for

Barcelona and gives Spain hope that it will become a factor in women's soccer in the future. Up until 2015, the Spanish team had never qualified for a World Cup, but with Maria, the future looks bright. Her goal against Canada in the U-20 World Cup—when she controlled the ball with her chest before burying it in the net—was named the goal of the tournament. Spain also beat Japan in that tournament.

Skill set: Speed. Good vision.

Breakout moment: At the U-20 World Cup, Maria's "goal of the tournament" helped Spain to a 5–0 win over Canada.

SANDRA OWUSU-ANSAH, GHANA
. . . .

Background: Sandra, born in 1997, played in both the U-17 and U-20 World Cups in 2016. The captain of her team, she scored a goal against the United States and could be instrumental in Ghana's potential future rise in women's soccer. The midfielder has already become famous in her own country.

Skill set: A solid offensive player, with a powerful shot, Owusu-Ansah can also mark the opposition's best player.

Breakout moment: Her curving goal from the top of the penalty box at the U-17 World Cup over Paraguay sent Ghana through to the quarterfinals.

GABI NUNES, BRAZIL

Background: Perhaps the heir apparent to Marta, the young striker scored five goals in four matches at the U-20 World Cup in 2016 when she was nineteen. A native of São Paulo, Gabi plays professionally in Brazil for Corinthians Audax. She also played for Brazil's U-17 team.

Skill set: Versatile and consistent. A nose for the goal.

Breakout moment: Gabi earned notice for her effective scoring at the U-20 World Cup, scoring five goals and tallying one assist in four matches.

DELPHINE CASCARINO, FRANCE

Background: The midfielder, who plays for Olympique Lyonnais, anchored the French U-20 team on its path to the World Cup final. Born in 1997, Delphine was the team captain and its primary stellar playmaker, both scoring and setting up goals. Some have accused her of being too unselfish, always looking to make the right pass. Her twin sister, Estelle, a defender, was also on the U-20 team and plays professionally in France for Juvisy.

Skill set: Good vision, passing and leadership.

Breakout moment: Her strike against defending champions Germany put France in the semifinal of the U-20 World Cup.

MYLENE CHAVAS, FRANCE

Background: When Mylene was just eighteen, she won the Golden Glove of the U-20 World Cup in 2016, signaling her emergence as a talented young goalkeeper to watch. She had three shutouts in the tournament including against powerful Germany. Born in 1998, Mylene plays professionally for Saint-Étienne.

Skill set: Strong with her feet, good with high balls. Confident and strong.

Breakout moment: Mylene recorded a shutout against defending champions Germany in the U-20 World Cup quarterfinals.

TOP TEN HIGHEST-RATED TELEVISED GAMES IN WOMEN'S SOCCER HISTORY

10.	JULY 10, 2011	USA VS. BRAZIL, WC QUARTER	3.89 MILLION
9.	AUG. 9, 2012	USA VS. JAPAN, OLYMPIC FINAL	4.35 MILLION
8.	JUNE 12, 2015	USA VS. SWEDEN, WC GROUP	4.5 MILLION
7.	JULY 4, 1999	USA VS. BRAZIL, WC SEMI	4.9 MILLION
6.	JUNE 16, 2015	USA VS. NIGERIA, WC GROUP	5.0 MILLION
5.	JUNE 26, 2015	USA VS. CHINA, WC QUARTER	5.7 MILLION
4.	JUNE 30, 2015	USA VS. GERMANY, WC SEMI	8.4 MILLION
3.	JULY 17, 2011	USA VS. JAPAN, WC FINAL	13.5 MILLION
2.	JULY 10, 1999	USA VS. CHINA, WC FINAL	17.9 MILLION
1.	JULY 6, 2015	USA VS. JAPAN, WC FINAL	25.4 MILLION

CHAMPIONS
OF
WOMEN'S
SOCCER

Abby Wambach's header ties the game in Team USA's 2011 Women's World Cup quarterfinal match against Brazil. (Thomas Eisenhuth/isiphotos.com)

Michelle Akers (center), Kristine Lilly (left), and Shannon MacMillan (right) celebrate the Americans' 1999 Women's World Cup semifinal victory over Brazil. (J. Brett Whitesell/isiphotos.com)

Kristine Lilly (USA) (left) fights for the ball against Andrea Neil (Canada) (right). (Michael Pimentel/isiphotos.com)

Brandi Chastain (second from left) hugs her teammates after scoring the game-winning penalty kick for Team USA in the 1999 Women's World Cup final. (J. Brett Whitesell/isiphotos.com)

Briana Scurry (USA) lunges toward the ball as she tries to make a save in a match against Mexico. (John Todd/isiphotos.com)

Hope Solo (USA) dives for a save in a game against China. (John Todd/isiphotos.com)

Marta (Brazil) (top) and Rachel Van Hollebeke (USA) (bottom) compete for possession of the ball in a 2011 Women's World Cup quarterfinal match. (Thomas Eisenhuth/isiphotos.com)

Homare Sawa (left) rejoices after scoring the game-tying goal for Japan in the 2011 Women's World Cup final against the USA. (Brad Smith/isiphotos.com)

Christine Sinclair (right) of the Portland Thorns shoots and scores in a National Women's Soccer League semifinal match against the Western New York Flash. (Craig Mitchelldyer/isiphotos.com)

Sun Wen (China) (right) dribbles the ball past Joy Fawcett (USA) (left) in the 1999 Women's World Cup final. (J. Brett Whitesell/isiphotos.com)

INDEX